Anonymous

Romanism, Protestantism and Anglicanism

Being a Layman's View of some Questions of the Day

Anonymous

Romanism, Protestantism and Anglicanism
Being a Layman's View of some Questions of the Day

ISBN/EAN: 9783744774666

Printed in Europe, USA, Canada, Australia, Japan

Cover: Foto ©Lupo / pixelio.de

More available books at **www.hansebooks.com**

A LAYMAN'S VIEW

OF

SOME QUESTIONS OF THE DAY

ROMANISM, PROTESTANTISM
ANGLICANISM

BEING

A LAYMAN'S VIEW of some QUESTIONS of the DAY

TOGETHER WITH REMARKS ON

DR. LITTLEDALE'S 'PLAIN REASONS AGAINST
JOINING THE CHURCH OF ROME'

BY

OXONIENSIS

LONDON
KEGAN PAUL, TRENCH, & CO., 1 PATERNOSTER SQUARE
1882

(The rights of translation and of reproduction are reserved)

PREFACE.

THE FOLLOWING PAGES are mainly the result of a careful study of Cardinal Newman's 'Apologia pro Vitâ suâ.' It is but seldom that a work which has taken its origin in a temporary and almost personal controversy retains a permanent interest or importance; but this appears to be an exception. The controversy which gave occasion to its publication may very well be forgotten, but the work itself will remain, not only the autobiography of one of the most interesting characters and probably the most influential theological writer of the century, but also the authentic record of the origin and early development of that great 'Oxford movement of 1833,' which has produced and continues to produce effects upon the Church of England of which no man living can expect to see the end.

In what follows I am concerned not with the temporary but with what I take to be the permanent importance of this remarkable book, and have endeavoured to point out what appears to be its argumentative value as regards the relations subsisting between certain important forms of Christian faith. That I have done this imperfectly and in outline only is, of course, true. To attempt anything more would be not only to go beyond the range of my own resources, but would require a volume so large as to be read but by few. Moreover, in dealing with theories professing to be historical, the production of but a few facts with which they are totally irreconcilable may suffice, if not to dispose of their claims to general acceptance, at least to induce persons who are interested in the subject to inquire for themselves before they admit them.

ROMANISM, PROTESTANTISM, ANGLICANISM.

CHAPTER I.

INTRODUCTORY.

THERE are many readers to whom an essay with such a title as the above will seem something utterly out of date. We are so often told that the question, now and for us, is, not whether one form of religion is better or worse than another, but whether any sort of religion at all can much longer hold its own as against thorough-going Atheism, that some of us are coming to think that a discussion of the former subject must be as stale and unprofitable as a recurrence to the arguments for and against the

Reform Act or the removal of the Jewish disabilities.

If I venture to dissent from this opinion it is certainly not because I under-estimate the importance of the issue which is at stake in the conflict between these two principles, nor yet because I have not studied the question, but rather because, having done so, I have failed to see that the case for Atheism is stronger than that for Theism, even upon purely intellectual grounds, while at the same time it is manifestly not upon intellectual grounds alone, or even chiefly, that the question, for the mass of mankind, will have to be decided.

In the words of the old Hebrew sage, 'the thing which hath been it is that which shall be.' Waves of Atheism have passed over the civilised world more than once in the course of its history, but the civilised world has nevertheless not become definitely or permanently Atheistic. Atheism has been for mankind nothing better than a kind of broken-down caravanserai. Men have from time to time attempted to take refuge in it, but the shelter which it affords is so precarious that few will ever remain there, and if they cannot come forth boldly into the king's highway of a God-fearing and man-regarding religion, they will slink out by the back door into the dark and filthy lanes of some miserable thaumaturgic superstition.

The present age of the world differs from its predecessors, not so much in the character of the changes which occur in it, as in their rapidity, and, though the tide of unbelief and no belief is at the present moment in full flood, signs are not wanting that a reaction of corresponding strength may shortly be looked for, and the character of that reaction may depend in no small degree upon the prevalence of true or false ideas and opinions on subjects for the present moment unfashionable and therefore unfamiliar. It should be remembered, too, that even at the present time, however much more interesting to the philosopher may be the discussion of the ultimate grounds of Theism or of Atheism, the great bulk of mankind and of society is but little affected by it. The personal interests and feelings of a vastly larger number of persons in this country are bound up rather with considerations of the conflicting claims of different forms of Christianity, than with the question of the truth or falsehood of Christianity altogether.

If this statement be once admitted, and it seems impossible to deny it, then it is clear that we shall find ample reason for such a discussion as I propose, if we look at the condition of Christianity from within instead of from without. Whether we take the Roman Church in this country or abroad, or the Protestant Churches in Germany, France, or Italy, or the Anglican Church, with its extension into the

Colonies and America, or the Disestablished Church in Ireland, or the Free Church in Scotland, or the countless nonconforming sects, even the most superficial observer cannot fail to see that the present century has witnessed great and very various changes among them.

Into the history of all these it would be quite unnecessary to enter, even were I competent to do it. It will be sufficient to refer in the briefest and most general terms to a few of the most remarkable of them. Thus, first of all, we have seen that great series of changes in the law which have consolidated religious liberty, commencing with the repeal of the Test Act and ending with the removal of the disabilities of the Jews. Then, in the Roman Church, we have seen the steady and gradual advance of the Jesuit and Ultramontane party, and its almost complete triumph over the old liberties of the Gallican and other national Churches, and the utter collapse of all attempts to ally it with modern liberalism, as, for example, by Montalembert and others in France, and by the writers in the 'Home and Foreign Review' in England. In Scotland we have seen the division of the two Churches, and the more recent and still repeated endeavours to attain to greater freedom of theological opinions within their bounds. In the Anglican communion, first the close of the Evangelical movement, then the rise and progress of the Tractarian and Ritualistic, with the various checks and counter-checks supplied by the Hampden and Gorham and Essayist prosecutions, and the innumerable conversions to Rome.

It is not possible that all these changes should have left the various bodies which have undergone them in exactly the same position in which they previously stood with reference either to each other or to the common foe without, and that they actually have not done so is obvious enough. Contrast for instance the claims of the Roman Catholic bishops when pleading for toleration before the Emancipation Act with those which they put forward now, or the tone of an Anglican divine when discoursing on the Sacraments before the days of Tract Ninety with that of the essays in 'The Church and the World,' and even many a less pronounced publication of recent years.

We may conclude, then, that there is nothing inopportune in discussing the relations of various forms of Christianity at the present time, since those relations are still unsettled; nor need such a discussion appeal to a small class of readers, since in reality it interests a far larger portion of mankind than do the more abstract and fundamental investigations lately become so popular, which would call into question the claims of Christianity and even of Theism altogether.

CHAPTER II.

IT is probably true that never, since the final re-establishment of the reformed religion in this country under Queen Elizabeth, has the reaction in favour of Church authority as against private judgment been so powerful as it is at the present moment. Under the Stuart sovereigns it was more immediately dangerous to the State and to social order, because while it was supported by the authority of the Crown, then vastly greater than it now is, it was associated also with political theories and practical oppressions which were alike hateful to the people; and partly also because the recollections of Smithfield and St. Bartholomew still kept their hold upon the minds and the imaginations of men, and 'Gunpowder Plot' had supplied a still more recent warning as to the spirit by which in those days such reaction was inspired. Hence, though more dangerous, it was less powerful: it tried its strength first under Laud then under James II., and failed utterly, and except for a short time during Anne's reign never became a serious power after the Revolution.

In our own day we have seen it revive with renewed strength after a long period of inaction, which has been sufficient not only to enable men to forget the hopes, fears, and feelings of their fathers, but almost to make them doubt whether such events as those just mentioned ever really took place, and why and by whom they were brought about. Into the causes of this reaction it is no part of my object to enter. Whether it be mere weariness of the perpetual conflicts and divisions of opinion to which private judgment gives rise, or dread of the consequences which have been or may be deduced from some of the theories to which it has led, or simple yielding to the force of the constantly reiterated claims of authority, and to the temptation of that tranquillity which is promised as the reward of admitting them; or whether it be a combination of all these causes and some others besides them to which we owe the fact—of the fact itself there can be no doubt, that in this country, after nearly three centuries of almost exclusive devotion to the principle of private judgment, we have been now for a whole generation in the midst of a still increasing reaction in favour of its opposite.

Let any person who is disposed to question this statement compare the tone adopted by Protestant writers within the last forty years with that assumed by them for a century and a half before, and his doubts will speedily vanish.

In the earlier of these two periods these

authors wrote not only with confidence in their cause but with a kind of assumption that the question was closed, that the verdict had been given decisively in their favour, and that the Roman Church was, as we should now say, 'played out.' Now, on the other hand, their tone is one of defence, almost of apology, as of an advocate who, whatever he may think of the goodness of his cause, is painfully conscious that the feeling of the jury is not in his favour.

Now since the facts of ecclesiastical history remain very much what they were, and since the arguments based on them must, one would suppose, have been very thoroughly threshed out after having employed most of the keenest intellects in Europe for the greater part of two centuries, no more striking proof could be given of the proposition so constantly suggested by Cardinal Newman, that in these matters men are guided far more by their sympathies than by their reason. But as we may still hope that reason is not altogether excluded from such questions, it may be worth while to restate in this place the several claims of authority and private judgment, and to trace out the position which they respectively hold towards the three systems of Christian belief with which we are to deal.

In so doing it will be well to refer constantly to the authority just mentioned, not only because Cardinal Newman has exercised an influence upon the present generation of Englishmen far beyond that of any other contemporary writer, but also because he himself professes to have passed in his own person through the stages of Protestantism and Anglicanism—of various degrees—before he found his ultimate rest in the system of the Roman Catholic Church. I use the word 'professes,' not because I would cast the slightest shadow of doubt upon Cardinal Newman's personal sincerity, but because I cannot perceive, judging from his own evidence in regard to himself, that he was ever really a Protestant. He received Protestant doctrines, but was never imbued with a really Protestant spirit. Even in his boyhood he concerned himself about 'dogma'[1] and 'celibacy' in a way which seems to show innate sympathies of quite a different kind, and from his earliest manhood his constant task appears to have been that of discovering where authority was to be found rather than whether it was to be found at all, and his constant aim since he reached his final position has been to reduce all questions such as those now under discussion to the single dilemma,[2] 'Romanism or Atheism: choose between them, for there is no intermediate standing ground.'

This conclusion is founded upon two propositions which it is the business of the 'Apologia' to prove and illustrate, not that it is true in a

---

[1] *Apologia pro Vitâ Suâ*, pp. 56-64.
[2] *Ibid.* pp. 322-23.

formal or controversial fashion, but in a way quite as instructive and far more interesting, viz. by means of a minute history of its author's religious opinions carried through all the phases which they have successively presented. These are,[1] (1) That some authority is necessary in order to withstand the solvent force of the human intellect; and (2) That no such authority is to be found, which will stand the test of experience and examination, elsewhere than in the Church of Rome. Let us examine these two premisses in some detail.[2] The former of them, or major premiss as it may be called, is little else than an assumption to which the author resorts under a sort of compulsion from the consideration of the generally unsatisfactory condition of the civilised world, and the destructive and disintegrating character of that Liberalism which he sees spreading everywhere and invading the province of religious no less than of political

[1] *Apologia*, p. 376.   [2] *Ibid.* pp. 67, 324.

and social life, which he defines as being 'the anti-dogmatic spirit,' and which he says repeatedly it was the main object of the Oxford movement of 1833 to withstand.[1] He bases it apparently on nothing more definite and tangible than the necessity for occupying some positive position, and the general probability that it might please the Creator of the Universe to interfere for the benefit of His perishing creatures, and that if He should so interfere it is not improbable that He should do so by introducing among them an infallible guide which should have authority to steer them through the winds and waves of this troublesome world.[2]

Throughout his book he is strong on the value of Butler's argument from probability (and, as was shown at the time by the Reviewer in 'Fraser's Magazine,'[3] he misapplies it in stating the *cumulative* force of the inducements to take

---

[1] *Apologia*, p. 195.   [2] *Ibid.* p. 382.
[3] See *Fraser's Magazine*, September 1864.

refuge in the Roman communion), and he thinks it excessively probable, considering the force of 'the wild living intellect of man,' that God 'should think fit to introduce a power into the world invested with the prerogative of infallibility in religious matters.'

It is somewhat remarkable in this connection, that while the ground of Butler's great work, viz. the nature of probable reasoning, and certain other matters which appear after all to be merely incidental to Butler's main argument—his inculcation of a visible Church, of the duties of external religion, and of the historical character of Revelation—appears to have struck Mr. Newman's mind very forcibly, the lesson which he draws from the argument which forms the scope and gives the name to the work is one which Butler himself, if I mistake not, never dreamed of.[1] He says 'the very idea of analogy between the separate works of God leads to the

[1] *Apologia*, p. 67.

conclusion that the system which is of less importance is economically or sacramentally connected with the more momentous system, and of this conclusion the theory to which I was inclined as a boy, viz. the unreality of material phenomena, is an ultimate resolution.'

Meanwhile assuredly the main scope of Butler's argument is something very different from all this, and might have sufficed of itself to lead him along quite a different road from that by which he has since travelled. Butler's argument was addressed to the Deists of the eighteenth century, to persons, that is, who admitted the existence of a God, and that He is the Author of Nature, but who denied the divine authority of Revelation, and he showed them how the difficulties in the way of Revelation, considered as coming from God, were very similar in character to those which are found in the order of nature, and that therefore, if the latter did not prevent their believing Him to be the Author of Nature, the former afforded an insufficient ground for denying that He was the Author of Revelation.

Few controversial treatises have met with more success and few theological arguments have been so generally pronounced to be conclusive as this was in its day and within the limits to which its author confined it. If we hear less of it now than we did fifty or thirty years ago, the reason is not that it has ceased to be a valid defence of the citadel of faith, but that the assault is now made upon an entirely different portion of the fortress.

There seems no reason why this main argument of Butler's should not be extended with force as well as fairness to the assumed probability of an infallible authority in religious matters.

In the whole system of nature there is nothing in the remotest degree analogous to an infallible authority. Even the lower animals, whose blind instincts are so much less liable to error than is the reason of man, sometimes make mistakes, and when they go wrong they suffer for it in the ordinary course of the laws of nature. There is no infallible guide to keep the hungry wolf out of the gin laid for him, or to warn the bird of the hidden gun ; and when we pass to man himself the same truth meets us at every turn—not only has he no infallible guide to warn him how to escape the death of the body—but neither has he any such to direct him in those moral and social perplexities which carry with them such important consequences to himself and others.

A father doubts how best to educate his son. He consults his own experience, he gets the best advice that he knows how to seek. He makes his decision with care and anxiety and prayer that it may be right. Yet he makes or may make a mistake upon which his son's whole future may depend. Surely this is a case in which an infallible guide is required as much as in determining what doctrines he is to believe, for the issues are at least as momentous. Yet none such is to be found. It is clearly no part of God's system of government in the one case: why should it be so in the other?

Look again at the thousand cases in which a thoughtful and conscientious man looks round at the circumstances in which he is placed, when he has to decide on some specific course of action, with a single eye to determining what is the line which his duty points out to him; and, long for an infallible guide as he may, no fire from heaven comes down upon his altar, 'there is no voice nor any to answer, neither any that regards him.' If he has faith he knows that God is just and merciful; he feels that the Judge of all the earth will do right, and trusts that all these trials and perplexities will in some way unknown to him work for his good, and, what is of more importance than all, he knows that all he has to do is to act honestly and without regard to his own interests or fears or wishes, and to leave the result in God's hands; but he knows well enough that he has no infallible guide to look to—that such is not the way in which God governs the world.

It is evident enough then that such an argument from probability as the one just quoted is demolished at once as soon as Butler's method is fairly applied to it; and indeed no reasoning can possibly be weaker than that which is drawn from a mere *à priori* probability of what the Deity may see fit to do as a means of effecting any particular object. At best it merely suggests that he who uses it is constructing a god in his own image, while at worst it becomes a mere makeshift argument, introduced to afford a plausible support to a feeble case.

It thus appears that Cardinal Newman's argument has not materially affected the considerations which can be adduced as against the theory that man can look for an infallible guide in matters of religion: all of these, whatsoever they may be, remain where they were before, only with the addition that the argument from analogy is shown to add greatly to their force.

To the discussion of this question it will be necessary to return by-and-by. In the meanwhile I propose to offer a few considerations upon what I may call Cardinal Newman's minor premiss, viz. that if there be an authoritative Church it is the Roman Church, and no other.

The argument in behalf of this is as follows. Authority may be of two kinds, or at least two theories of it have been propounded, viz. (1) That there is an actual organised Church which has definite and plenary powers; that this Church is the same now in authority and in power as it was in the days of the apostles; that it has now as it had then the duty and the power of defining articles of faith, so that the doctrine of the immaculate conception propounded under Pio Nono is as much a part of the Christian faith now, and stands on the same authority, as does that of the incarnation itself. This, shortly and imperfectly expressed, is the Roman theory.

Then there is another,[1] viz. (2) that which takes up what it is pleased to call primitive authority, or the authority of the early councils and fathers, and will receive their opinions as authoritative, if not infallible, in all cases of doubt; the theory being, not that an individual father, say St. Augustine, is himself infallible, but that he is a competent witness to what was the authoritative teaching of the primitive Church.[1] This is the high Anglican theory, and it is at first sight plausible enough. The objections to it are, however, serious: some of them are admirably brought out in the *Apologia*, esp. pp. 191–216 and

[1] See Hook's *Church Dictionary*, art. 'Fathers.'

pp. 320-36. They may be summarised thus: Besides the general question, Where are you to draw your line as to what is antiquity and what not? there is the further point that wherever you do draw it you will find evidence above it for doctrines which the Anglican Church rejects, and evidence below it for some which it accepts.[1] It thus fails in both directions, for the same objections lie against some of its beliefs which Protestants urge against Rome, while in reference to others Romanists can allege against it that it rejects 'doctrines and usages which have ever been received in the East and West.'[2]

Cardinal Newman contrasts the two theories under the titles of the argument from Catholicity and the argument from Antiquity, and shows very strikingly the weakness of the latter, in a passage in which he quotes St. Augustine's condemnation of the Donatists. He says of the

[1] *Apologia*, pp. 321-2.   [2] *Ibid.* pp. 197-8.

words, *securus judicat orbis terrarum*, 'they decided ecclesiastical questions on a simpler rule than that of antiquity; nay, St. Augustine was one of the prime oracles of antiquity; here, then, was antiquity deciding against itself.'[1] And indeed this passage suggests a very obvious, but a somewhat formidable argument against antiquity, which might perhaps be called the argument from perspective.

It seems as if persons who use arguments from antiquity, in whatever sense, and for whatever purpose, were peculiarly liable to lose all sense of the *relative* value of different times, or persons, or works; as if they lost their sense of perspective, and could not tell with any certainty the relation in which objects stand towards one another. Just as a child, if you take him out in a fine summer night, and point out to him, first the moon, and then Jupiter, will tell you that the moon is ever

[1] *Apologia*, 211–12.

so much the biggest; or as a savage, when he has counted up to four or five, loses all definite notion of number, and takes refuge in some phrase expressive of an indefinite multitude; so do a vast number of persons use the words 'antiquity,' 'ancient,' 'primitive,' &c., as if they stood for absolute, instead of merely relative, ideas.

Thus, to take the instance at present before us, St. Augustine, 'one of the prime oracles of antiquity,' as Cardinal Newman very justly calls him, belongs to the latter end of the fourth Christian century, and took a leading part in all the controversies of his time. Yet we are asked to accept his views of what was the belief and practice of the Church three hundred years before, and nobody seems struck with the absurdity of this. It is as if we should accept the evidence of Lord Macaulay on the political controversies of the Tudor times, or that of Cardinal Newman himself on the religious disputes of the same period. We should listen to it indeed with much interest, as to the testimony of some of the ablest men of our time, treating of subjects to which they had given much attention and devoted great powers ; but to appeal to such men as impartial witnesses in regard to the real beliefs, opinions, or practices of the statesmen and divines of those times, is what none but the greatest ignoramus or the wildst partisan would dream of proposing.

Carry the comparison just a little further. Look at what has happened, say, between the middle of the sixteenth century and the middle of the nineteenth. The great Protestant Reformation under Edward VI., the reaction and persecution under Mary, the establishment of the English Church under Queen Elizabeth, the reaction under Laud in Charles I.'s reign, the Rebellion and temporary overthrow of the Church, its re-establishment under Charles II.; the various controversies, the enactment and repeal of penal statutes against Roman Catholics and Nonconformists, which occupied the latter end of the seventeenth and most of the eighteenth centuries; the Methodist movement, the Evangelical movement, the removal of religious disabilities, and finally, the great Oxford movement under Mr. Newman himself.

Of all these important occurrences, and innumerable smaller ones, we have plentiful accounts, but no one supposes that they have left their marks on paper only, or that the men actually engaged in each different stage of them can be unaffected and impartial witnesses in regard to the previous ones. In time, Cardinal Newman himself bears the same relation to Archbishop Cranmer that St. Augustine does to St. Paul, yet who would take him as an impartial judge of the doctrines and views of the great Reforming prelate? And the further we carry the comparison, the more striking does it appear. Not only is the lapse of time in the first case as great as in the second, but important to the Church as are the occurrences which have taken place in the last three centuries, no one could pretend that those in the first three were not more important still; for no event since the Reformation can be reckoned of importance at all commensurate with the Christianizing of the Roman Empire and the assembling of the Council of Nicæa. Moreover, it is not only the differing circumstances of his own time which place a great man of one period out of sympathy with one of another, there is also to be taken into consideration the imperfection of his knowledge as to what were the real feelings and thoughts of the other. He gets them through the reports of several generations of witnesses, themselves imperfectly informed, prejudiced, interested in maintaining one view rather than another; and even when he reads the writings of the earlier author himself, he reads them with imperfect light, from the scantiness of his information as to the circumstances under which they were written and the shades of feeling which dictated them.

And if this is the case, as we see it to be, when dealing with writers of the last three centuries, with all the aids of printing presses and libraries and continuous literary history, how much more must it have been so in the case of the first three centuries, amidst the difficulties occasioned by want of libraries and printing, by comparatively rare and difficult intercourse between one place and another, with all the superadded obstacles occasioned by diversities of race and language! Yet while every even partially educated person would receive with the utmost reserve the evidence of an English divine of the nineteenth century as to the views of one of the sixteenth, multitudes are ready to swallow without question or hesitation that of a fourth-century father in regard to the beliefs and usages of the primitive Church. We know well enough that the last three Christian centuries have afforded ample time for beliefs, usages, customs, institutions, sects, and factions to rise, to develop, to flourish, to decay, to degenerate, to disappear, and to reappear in forms which their authors would fail to recognise; why, then, should we believe that all these things remained stationary in the no less stirring times of the first three, unless it is because they are so lost in the dim distance of antiquity that we have ceased to see anything clearly about them at all?

It is thus evident that antiquity as a mode of Church authority breaks down altogether. There is no possibility of settling, on any rational grounds, a point at which antiquity ceases to be authoritative. Wherever we attempt to fix such a point, it will be inconsistent with the particular selection of doctrines which the Anglican Church, or at least the High Church section of it, has received or has rejected; and further, it would be a difficult or an impossible thing to settle beyond dispute exactly which of these had been accepted by the Church at the period selected as the limit of authoritative antiquity.

That both these last two statements cannot be false, though both may be true, is proved to demonstration by the following short passage in the 'Apologia.'[1] The author says, quoting an earlier writing of his own: 'The proof of the Roman (modern) doctrine is as strong (or stronger) in antiquity, as that of certain doctrines which both we and the Romans hold; *e.g.* there is more of evidence in antiquity for the necessity of Unity, than for the Apostolical Succession; for the supremacy of the See of Rome, than for the Presence in the Eucharist; for the practice of Invocation, than for certain books in the present Canon of Scripture, &c. &c.'

[1] *Apologia*, pp. 321-2.

Now, from this statement there is no escape. It can but be true or not true. If it is true, it shows that the High Anglicans have drawn their line of antiquity in an indefensible place; and if it is not true, it proves the impossibility of determining what is really to be found above and what below that line.

Again, the whole history of antiquity would tend to show, if we could but rid ourselves of that process of intellectual foreshortening just now described, (1) that the fourth and fifth centuries have no real claims upon the reverence of posterity, for not only, as we have seen, was there ample time for the men of those centuries to have lost much of the tradition, as well as of the spirit of the earlier days of Christianity, but there exists ample evidence to show that they had done so as a fact. Witness the intrigues in connection with the so-called Robber Council, the discreditable violence of the Bishops at Chalcedon, and the double-dealing and insincerity traceable even among the venerable fathers of Nicæa.[1] (2) That if we set these aside and go only to the still earlier ages of the Church, we are driven to a theory of development in some form in order to account for such doctrines as those above mentioned. Even so sober a writer as Canon Robertson[2] admits this, though he fails, as indeed he could not but fail, to show how, if development is once admitted, it can stop short of a justification of the doctrines of modern Rome; once admit that any authority has existed, in so-called primitive times, which could legitimately develop doctrine, and the argument from thence to the modern Roman Church is like a chain of adamant—there is no

---

[1] See Milman's *Latin Christianity*, vol. i. pp. 95-6, and 201 *et seq.*; also Stanley's *Lectures on the Eastern Church*, Lect. II., and Stanley's *Christian Institutions*, pp. 322 *et seq.*, where he quotes Cardinal Newman.

[2] Robertson's *Church History*, vol. i. p. 81.

link to which you can point which is not stronger than the first.

The belief in what is called primitive Christianity, in what Newman once spoke of as 'ancient, holy, and happy times,' attractive as it is, has no historical basis whatever, and must be consigned to the same limbo as those older myths of a golden age which it somewhat resembles. It is founded not on the history which we know, but on the history which we do not know—on our ignorance, not on our knowledge; and wherever we are able to substitute the latter for the former, there we find that no golden age exists, though the belief is general that it once existed.

The supposition that any institution whatever can exist among men for two or three centuries together without undergoing change and corruption, is a contradiction to all experience. And this contradiction is not removed in the case of the Christian Church by a reference to its divine origin. We happen to have, in the Jewish Church, an instance of another institution confessedly also of divine origin, and in this case the books which contain its history are among the writings held sacred by Christians, yet those sacred writings assure us that that divinely appointed institution had sunk into the very lowest depths of corruption and degradation within fifty years after the death of Moses, according to the commonly received chronology.

The history of the Church of England itself also affords the same lesson from another point of view. Its system was supposed to be perfected once for all some 300 years ago, and has, as far as its authoritative documents go, undergone no change for at least 200 years. The result can hardly be considered satisfactory, for none of the parties within it are really in harmony with all of these. Twice[1] within the

[1] *Tracts for the Times*, xc., and Mr. Wilson's Essay in *Essays and Reviews*.

lifetime of the present generation we have seen elaborate treatises published for the purpose of proving either that the Articles have no signification at all, or that it is not what their framers designed it to be. They do not prevent members and ministers of the Church from holding contradictory doctrines; and for generations past they have owed their continued existence, not to any reverence or affection in which they are held, but simply to the well-founded dread that if once they were touched, the dissensions following would be such that the whole organism of the Anglican Church would dissolve into its constituent elements.

Cardinal Newman, then, has fairly established his minor premise, and in so doing he has utterly wrecked the High Anglican theory, and it is only one more among the innumerable examples of how little argument has to do with belief in the greatest part of mankind that that theory, raised as it was from the merest insignificance mainly by his own efforts, should so long have survived his desertion and his assault. It must be noticed, however, in this connection, that there could be no greater mistake than to suppose that it was only from the side of the Church of Rome, or of Cardinal Newman's argument from catholicity, that the Anglican theory and the argument from antiquity have been assailed with success. The ripest learning and the most judicial mind in the service of the Church of England herself, in the person of the present Bishop of Durham, have pronounced decisively against the claim, whether by the Anglican or any other church, to support a sacerdotal theory of any kind upon the evidence of primitive antiquity, not only affording, from an exhaustive examination of the earliest Christian writers, the negative proof of mere silence as to any such claim until quite the close of the second century, but showing also that this silence is maintained exactly where the writer's purpose would have been best attained by the help of such a doctrine, had it been in existence, or had he believed it.[1]

It will be remembered in the history of controversy, that the early partisans of the Oxford movement of 1833 constantly reproached the evangelical clergy with ignorance, and especially of the patristic writers, and that they have posed ever since as the learned clergy, *par excellence.* That there was some truth in the charge there can be no doubt, and the party which brought it obtained a vast controversial advantage by so doing; for their opponents, being quite unable to meet them on their own ground at the time, the public came to believe that the fathers were universally on their side. It should have been remembered, however, that the evangelical clergy were the working clergy of the day, and had at any rate the same excuse for their ignorance of the fathers which a

[1] Lightfoot on *Philippians,* pp. 243 *et seq.*

working lawyer might allege for his ignorance of Justinian or Gaius, or a practising doctor for his non-acquaintance with Galen, viz. that, great as their authority had been in its day, it had been in fact superseded.

The parallel is in truth more exact than might be supposed, for the divines of the Reformation period had been thoroughly familiar with the fathers, and at the very same time that they used them with telling effect against their Romanist opponents, had in fact superseded their authority, by the narrow limit to which they confined it, as in the well-known words of Œcolampadius : 'If we quote the fathers, it is only to free our doctrine from the reproach of novelty, not to support our cause by their authority.'[1] Accordingly, we find two curious results, which, however, the history of the Reformation might fairly have led us to expect, viz. (1) that, as we have just seen from two

[1] D'Aubigné's *Ref.*, vol. iv. p. 113.

opposite sources of information, patristic learning, when real, so far from supporting the Anglican theory, shows it to be untenable ; and, consequently, (2) that we hear a good deal less about such learning now, from the chiefs of the party, and that its rank and file have long ceased to be conspicuous for learning of any kind.

CHAPTER III.

THE next step in our argument will be to show that almost every doctrine and every practice which distinguishes High Anglicanism from Protestantism is a mere reversion to the old doctrines or practices of Rome; to things, that is to say, which have no justification, no meaning, no intelligible *raison d'être* apart from Rome, which were cast off at the Reformation as the very badges of Rome, and the resumption of which is at once a repudiation of the Reformation and a confession of the illegitimacy of the English Church.

Take, for instance, the doctrine of the Apostolical succession. And here it is necessary to remind my readers of what some even well-informed persons are apt to forget, viz. that the phrase Apostolical succession stands for two totally distinct ideas. It stands primarily for a belief that as a simple matter of historical fact there has been preserved an uninterrupted succession of ordained persons from the time of the apostles to the present day. But it also stands, in the second place, for a theological doctrine, based on this historical belief, and bound up inextricably with what is called the high sacramental doctrine, viz. that bishops and priests so ordained, and by virtue of that uninterrupted succession alone, can ordain others to succeed them, and can impart efficacy to the sacramental ordinances of the Church.

Now, it is clear that the doctrine cannot stand without its historical basis, and that the historical theory, though true, would be unimportant but for the doctrine which it supports. Of the historical theory it is only certain that it cannot be *proved*. It would be as impossible to demonstrate to the satisfaction of a modern critical historian that Linus and Cletus were the second and third Bishops of Rome, as that Numa and Tullus were the second and third Kings of Rome. To persons not more than ordinarily sceptical, it will doubtless appear that both assertions are more probable than not, and that the asserted succession of the Christian bishops is the more likely to be historical of the two; still, most persons would feel that if a man's title to an office or an estate depended on the due performance of some official act by Numa Pompilius, its safety would in fact rest solely on the impossibility that any rival claimant could make out a better one. But let the probability be granted; and since 'probability is the guide of life,' let us follow it in this case.

Then, again, of the doctrine which is founded on this historical theory, the one thing which can be safely asserted is that it is not, and never has been, the doctrine of the

Church of England. The proof of this is so easy, the fact is so obvious, that it is only by carefully ignoring and keeping out of sight the whole history of that Church for the first century of her separate existence, and a portion of one of the most important charters on which she has relied since that time, that the opposite opinion can be rendered even plausible.

There are two sources of evidence from which we may judge whether the Church of England has really held this doctrine or not, viz. first, her practice; and secondly, her theory.

With regard to the former there can be very little doubt. The evidence of a witness at once so competent and so unwilling as the late Mr. Keble may be held sufficient,[1] and he says plainly that during Elizabeth's reign ' numbers of persons were admitted to the ministry of the Church in England with no better than Presby-

---

[1] Keble, *Preface to Hooker*, p. lxxvi.

terian ordination;' and similar irregularities were constantly repeated until the Restoration. Even Lancelot Andrews,[1] the extremest of High Churchmen, as High Churchmen were then reckoned, took part in consecrating, as bishops for Scotland, men who never had received episcopal ordination as priests.

So far, then, as doctrine can be judged from practice, these instances are sufficient to show what the practice really was. It may indeed be said that you cannot argue from practice to theory, that neither individuals nor churches could afford to be judged according to so stringent a test, and this is doubtless true; but when we consider what is implied by holding the doctrine of the Apostolical succession, and largely neglecting it in practice, I think but few loyal members of the English Church would thank her advocates for saving her orthodoxy

---

[1] Spotswoode, *History of the Church of Scotland*, vol. iii. pp. 210-11, edit. 1851.

on this point at the price of admitting such a charge—for it could mean nothing less than that the Church had deliberately left whole congregations and whole parishes for generations, nay for centuries together, without valid sacraments or other rites, and in all important respects in the condition of excommunicated persons or of communities under an interdict. Such an admission would be a heavy price to pay even for the purpose of sustaining an orthodox theory. But can the theory be sustained after all?

The sources from which we can judge of the theory of a church are (1) its articles and formularies; (2) in the case of a State church at least, any Acts of Parliament relating to it; and (3) the statements or writings of its accredited controversialists. Now where the practice is, as in this case, in flagrant contradiction to the asserted theory, these authorities ought to be unmistakable if the theory is to be maintained at all; and so indeed they are, but not exactly in the sense which its supporters require. Two out of the three possible authorities may be dismissed in a single sentence, for there is simply not a single word about the matter in the articles and formularies, and as regards Acts of Parliament, the thirteenth of Elizabeth, by which non-episcopal ordination was always held to be legitimated, remained in force during the whole period in question.

We come, then, in the last resort to the controversialists. Now without a doubt the accredited champions of the Church of England in Elizabeth's reign were Jewell, Whitgift, and Hooker. Of these Jewell utterly repudiates episcopal authority, except as a matter of discipline.[1] Whitgift says plainly,[2] 'The bishops of the realm do not (so far as I ever yet heard)

---

[1] Jewell's works, *Jelf*, vol. iv. pp. 433 and 481, in the '*Defence of the Apologia.*'

[2] See *Life*, by Strype, vol. iii. pp. 222-3.

nor must not claim to themselves any greater authority than is given to them by the statute of the 25th of King Henry VIII., revived in the first year of Her Majesty's reign, or by other statutes of the land, neither is it reasonable that they should make other claims. *For if it had pleased Her Majesty with the wisdom of the realm, to have used no bishops at all, we could not have complained justly of any defect in our Church*;' and again, 'For if it had pleased Her Majesty to have assigned the imposition of hands to the Deans of every Cathedral Church or some other number of ministers which in no sort were bishops, but as they be pastors, there had been no wrong done to their persons that I can conceive.' Hooker, as is well known, is claimed as a champion by the partisans on both sides of the controversy.[1] It is sufficient to remark of him that his great work was written expressly against the Puritans, that he is mani

---

[1] *Hooker*, Bk. III., xi. 8 and 16, pp. 391 and 409

festly most desirous throughout to claim all he can of authority for episcopacy, yet that his latest editor is quite unable, though most anxious, to adduce from his writings anything like an unqualified statement in favour of the doctrine of Apostolical succession, and is compelled to admit the genuineness of passages acknowledging in some cases at least the validity of nonepiscopal orders.

On the other hand, the whole history of the times, the lives of Parker and Jewell and their contemporaries and immediate successors, and the nature of their relations with the leading men of the reformed churches on the Continent, serve to show that while some of them valued episcopacy highly as the best authenticated and most convenient form of church government, and others looked upon it as little better than a necessary evil, all alike viewed it as a matter of government and discipline only. They do not appear to have troubled themselves with the consideration of whether they had the succession as a matter of fact, but simply gave it up as a matter of doctrine.

Mr. Keble somewhat naïvely remarks in regard to these writers, 'It is enough, with them, to show that the government by Archbishops and Bishops is ancient and allowable; they never venture to urge its *exclusive* claim or to connect the succession with the validity of the Holy Sacraments, and yet it is obvious that such a course of argument alone (supposing it borne out by facts) could fully meet all the exigencies of the case. It must have occurred to the learned writers above mentioned, since it was the received doctrine of the Church down to their days; and if they had disapproved it, as some theologians of no small renown have since done, it seems unlikely that they should have passed it over without express avowal of dissent; considering that they always wrote with an eye to the pretensions of Rome also, which popular opinion had in a great degree mixed up with the doctrine of Apostolical succession.'[1]

This argument is plainly double-edged. It is at least as probable an explanation of their silence that they did not 'urge' the doctrine because they did not hold it, because they too shared the 'popular opinion' that it was in fact a Romish doctrine. If they had held it, and connected with it 'the validity of the Holy Sacraments,' how could they ever have permitted unordained persons (*i.e.* non-episcopally ordained) to minister as they constantly did? But the matter is beyond the range of discussion. I will only ask: If a man engaged in a controversy omits to use the most obvious and conclusive argument of which his case admits, and the hypothesis of ignorance is excluded, is the inference from his so doing that he *does not* dissent from it? or that he *does* dissent from it,

---

[1] *Preface to Hooker*, p. lix.

and therefore cannot use it? Controversialists are not generally in any great haste to 'avow dissent' from the only argument which can 'fully meet the exigencies' of their case; and if, as Mr. Keble no doubt rightly insists, these writers could not have been ignorant of the doctrine of the Apostolical succession, and yet abstained from urging it, it must follow either that they did so because, as I maintain, they did not hold it, or else that they abstained from producing the grounds on which they themselves held their conclusions, because they feared they were unpopular. I believe that they were much too sincere and honest men to do this, and even were they not, their opponents would hardly have failed to bring the charge against them at the time. But in fact no Roman controversialist of that day would ever have suspected a Protestant opponent of holding such a doctrine, and therefore it is a fair assumption in any case, that if such a person, as

Mr. Keble expressly admits, did not allege it, it was because he did not believe it.

There may be a *shadow* of a doubt as to the fact, that is, as to whether Parker's consecration was strictly regular, since no record is to be found of Barlows, by whom he was consecrated;[1] but there is no doubt at all that Parker and his immediate successors, as well as most of his contemporary bishops, were absolutely indifferent as to whether they had the succession or not.[2] But perhaps the most conclusive of all considerations as to the position which the English Church occupies in regard to this question is to be found in the facts that (1) up to the year 1820, *i.e.* the end of George III.'s reign, a large proportion of the clergy in the Channel

---

[1] See Hunt's *History of Religious Thought in England*, vol. i. p. 42, *note*. A work of great value for purposes of reference.

[2] On this whole subject, see an able letter entitled *Apostolical Succession not a Doctrine of the Church of England*, by Cantab (Longmans, 1870), in which it is fully discussed from the Romish point of view.

Islands were not episcopally ordained, although they ministered according to the formularies of the Church of England, and formed a part of the clergy of the diocese of Winchester; (2) that the kings of England up to the same date constantly had attached to their households a Presbyterian chaplain; (3) that the Queen to this day has the same in Scotland; and (4) that the Act of Uniformity of Charles II.—the very Act and the first and only Act which made it necessary as a rule that all persons thereafter to be admitted to the cure of souls in England should have been episcopally ordained—contains also a clause[1] specially permitting the king to admit persons not so ordained, who were foreigners and ordained in the foreign Protestant churches, according to the usages of those churches, to preferments

[1] 'Provided that the penalties in this Act shall not extend to the foreigners or aliens of the Foreign Reformed Churches allowed or to be allowed by the King's Majesty his heirs or successors in England.'

in the English Church without re-ordination. This permissive clause was acted upon by King Charles II. within a very few years after it was passed, and it would doubtless be within the powers of her present Majesty to act upon it again if she should see fit to do so.

This being the actual position of the English Church from the reign of Elizabeth to the present time, it is nothing less than an absurdity to talk of it as holding the 'doctrine of the Apostolical succession.'

There are, of course, other arguments which are used, and used very effectively, by Roman controversialists, which are amply sufficient to show that the doctrine of Apostolical succession, even if the English Church held it, would avail it nothing, as, for instance, that derived from the fact that Arians, Donatists, heretics, and schismatics of all sorts and conditions have held the doctrine, as well as possessed the succession in fact, and have been heretics and schismatics none the less; but what I am more anxious to point out is the utterly worthless character of the claim itself as put forth by the English High Church party. Not that it is one of doubtful validity which might afford a good ground for discussion, and so a fair excuse for believing the other High Church theories based upon it, but that it is utter pinchbeck and rubbish from beginning to end, resembling nothing in secular life so much as the late Tichborne claim, and, like it, has been nursed into factitious importance by the interests of a few and the ignorance of many. And, indeed, the interest involved is a heavy one, for without this doctrine the whole sacerdotal claim and all that depends upon it comes down with a crash. This doctrine of the Apostolical succession, which some people are apt thoughtlessly to admit as a polite concession to clerical susceptibilities, in the same way as they would abstain from contesting a Scotchman's claim to descent from William Wallace or Fingal, is, of course, theologically considered, of the utmost and most real importance, because without it, as High Churchmen themselves are constrained to admit, the whole of the distinctively 'high' doctrine in regard to the sacraments and the power of the keys, &c., falls to the ground, though it is not equally certain that the converse is true.

A similar line of argument is equally applicable to the doctrine of the Eucharist. A claim is now put forth by many of the High Church clergy to hold and to teach a doctrine which is to ordinary minds quite undistinguishable from that of Rome, yet nothing is more certain than these three propositions : (1) That Cranmer and the other bishops under Edward VI., who themselves drew up the Articles, held Calvinistic, if not Zwinglian doctrine on this subject ; (2) that it was for this doctrine, not less than for rejecting the Pope's supremacy, that they and their fellows were burnt; and (3) that on the re-establishment of the English Church under Elizabeth, Parker, Jewell, and their fellows again recurred to Zwinglian doctrine.

In the writings of these men, and of their contemporaries on one side or the other, there is simply no room for mistake on this subject. The doctrine of 'the Mass' is the one main and wide distinction between Rome and Protestantism, which cannot be got over. 'Does he allow the Mass?' is the first question asked by either side when they wish to learn under what colours a fresh disputant or an applicant for favour is prepared to sail. Cranmer and Ridley drew up the Articles on the Eucharist not four years before they were burnt for the doctrine which they held in regard to it, and they arranged and sanctioned the Communion Office in Edward VI.'s Prayer-book. It is clear, therefore, that they did not look upon the latter as incompatible with the former, nor is it credible that they were so in love with martyrdom as to permit themselves to be burnt for holding a doctrine which was after all indistinguishable from that of their judges.

Before proceeding further, there is a peculiarity of the High Church writers which calls for a brief notice. These writers have an almost universal habit, when they appeal to the authority of Anglican divines at all, of referring almost exclusively to authors of the seventeenth century.[1] Why they should do so, if they are permitted, is obvious enough. If they are merely advocates of a cause which they intend to support, sound or unsound, then they are quite right to choose those authors and set them up as authorities who will lend, at any rate, a partial and modified support to that cause, but why in the world their opponents should have permitted them to do it, or how any one should have been deceived by so trans-

[1] *Apologia*, pp. 113, 120, 140.

parent an artifice, it is really difficult to understand.

Whether we look at it from the point of view of the authors themselves, their position, their means of knowledge, their character, their experiences, the sufferings which they were called upon to endure for their cause; or whether we consider the actual facts in the history of the Church of England, and their bearing upon modern ecclesiastical claims made in her behalf, it seems as impossible to deny the superiority in importance of the Acts of Henry, Edward, Mary, and Elizabeth, to those of the Stuarts, as the personal superiority of Ridley, Jewell, and Hooker to such persons as Bancroft, Sheldon, and Samuel Parker. To take a parallel case from modern history, what should we think of the honesty or of the intelligence of a man who, proposing to investigate what the French call the principles of 1789, should invoke as his authorities the speculations of Louis Blanc, Michelet, or Victor Hugo, instead of going to the fountain head and consulting the actual lives, speeches, and writings of the actors in the Great Revolution?

Either the Church of England has maintained an ecclesiastical, as distinguished from a Protestant character and theory, or it has not. There may be and are, as we all know, innumerable disputes as to the fact; but one thing must be plain to the understanding of every intelligent person, viz. this, that the change, if change there was, took place in the sixteenth century, not in the seventeenth; and that if the ecclesiastical theory and practice was given up in the sixteenth century, it could not be re-assumed in the next, so that in any case the question must be decided, if at all, upon the evidence of the former century alone. The history of the matter appears to be shortly this, that the reformers and the bishops of the English Church were as purely and simply Protestant as were the ministers of the German, French, Dutch, and Swiss Reformed Churches, from the beginning of Edward VI.'s reign down to nearly the end of Elizabeth's; though in the last years of the latter reign a few divines, the most important of whom were Bilson and Bancroft, began to set up a claim of divine right for episcopacy mainly as it would seem as a makeweight against the similar claim of the Presbyterians in favour of their 'discipline.'[1] Of this doctrine Whitgift is reported to have said that 'he did not believe it to be true, but he wished it were.'[2]

From this time, with that curious tendency which extreme opinions seem to have to generate their opposites, as Puritanism advanced so *pari passu* did ecclesiasticism advance; but it was not until Laud became its leader, and was promoted to be successively Bishop of

---

[1] See *Hooker*, Lib. III. ch. ii. 2.
[2] Hunt's *Hist. of Religious Thought*, &c., vol. i. p. 86.

London and Archbishop of Canterbury, that it became for the time predominant in the Church. Its history from that time is remarkable and interesting, both for the coincidences and contrasts which it affords to that of its revival in our own days—but these cannot be pursued here. It is sufficient to recall how in Laud's time the scent of the fires of Smithfield and Oxford was still too strong in the nostrils of the English people to leave them any relish for the re-establishment of Popery, even without the Pope; and his enterprise had no small share in bringing about the common ruin of the Church and the monarchy. The reign of Puritanism followed, and in its turn quickly brought about its own destruction. Then came the Restoration, when, under the baneful influence of Charles II. and Gilbert Sheldon, the most intolerant section of the clergy had the upper hand, and all Laud's pretensions were renewed; though throughout, even amongst those who were reckoned in the number of his especial partisans, some were to be found, such as Cosin,[1] who were purely Protestant when they could not help it.

But the most singular stage in the history of this earliest development of High Churchism in the Church of England is the concluding one. James II. came to the throne and avowed himself a Roman Catholic, and then—not quite all at once, but in a very short time—it was seen that the Anglican divines, though they were willing enough to use Romanist arguments against Nonconformists, and to enhance their own dignity and importance by insisting on Apostolical succession and episcopacy by divine right, were compelled, when driven to the choice between Protestantism and Romanism pure and simple, to drop their sham Catholicism, and come forth to the light as unmistakably Protestant as Cranmer or Parker. In particular, the various authors whose

[1] Hunt, *op. cit.* vol. i. p. 303.

writings are collected together in the work known as 'Gibson's Preservative,'[1] gave up the doctrine of Apostolical succession altogether, and expressly admitted the validity of non-episcopal orders. No doubt was then left on the minds of men that the English Church was essentially Protestant, and that her episcopacy was a question of church government only, and not to be reckoned as one of the necessary characters of a church.

Thus is the saying with which the Bishop of London scandalised Mr. Newman in 1833 a very simple statement of an equally simple historical fact, that 'belief in the apostolical succession went out with the non-jurors.' It did so go out, and the Church of England has little reason to thank Mr. Newman and his friends by whose efforts alone it has been galvanised into an unwholesome life again.

There can be no doubt that the whole

[1] Hunt, *op. cit.* vol. ii. pp. 29 *et seq.*

sacerdotal theory and the high sacramental doctrine as depending upon it, hangs upon the Apostolical succession—not, that is, directly upon the fact, if fact it be, but upon the doctrine of the Apostolical succession; that both alike were thrown overboard by the English Church in the reigns of Edward VI. and Elizabeth; and that the Church as a church has made no attempt since that time to resume them; though there has always since Bancroft's time been a party—which, induced either by the pressure of controversy with Nonconformists, or by the desire to increase the influence of the clergy, has made frantic efforts, in the teeth of all the facts of history, and the whole spirit and *rationale* of the Reformation, and the strongest prejudices and deepest feelings of the nation, to re-establish them.

And why these doctrines should have been given up, and why they should not be resumed, even if upon any coherent Church theory resumption of them were possible, is evident enough, among many other reasons especially for this, that once admit them, and the Church of England ceases to have any longer a *raison d'être*. For these, if they are anything at all, must be everything, must be of the very essence of the Church; they must be what makes it necessary to be within the Church. Plainly you cannot drop them to-day and take them up again to-morrow, nor can you with any safety separate from the Church which confessedly possesses them.

It is strange that Anglican theorists determinately refuse to learn the lesson which Cardinal Newman has so forcibly impressed upon them, that they will not see that the more they minimise the differences between themselves and Rome, the more untenable becomes their own position. The Anglican Church, as a fact, is separate from Rome, is repudiated, disowned, anathematised by Rome; and hence it is plain that unless the differences between them be weighty and even vital, it has no valid excuse for being outside her pale. To put the matter shortly, and in more technical language, since there is such a thing as schism, as well as heresy, it must follow from the above considerations that if Rome be not heresy, Anglicanism must be schism. No words can express more forcibly or more truly the untenableness of the Anglican position than these which Cardinal Newman has quoted in the 'Apologia,' from an earlier writing of his own:[1] 'A man who can set down half a dozen general propositions, which escape from destroying one another only by being diluted into truisms, who can hold the balance between opposites so skilfully as to do without fulcrum or beam, who never enunciates a truth without guarding himself against being supposed to exclude the contradictory, who holds that Scripture is the only authority, yet that the

[1] *Apologia*, p. 193.

Church is to be deferred to; that faith only justifies, yet that it does not justify without works; that grace does not depend on the sacraments, yet is not given without them; that bishops are a divine ordinance, yet those that have them not are in the same condition as those who have—this is your safe man and the hope of the Church; this is what the Church is said to want, not party men, but sensible, temperate, sober, well-judging persons, to guide it through the channel of no-meaning—between the Scylla and Charybdis of aye and no.' And later events seem rapidly bringing to pass his further prediction that men 'cannot go on for ever standing on one leg, or sitting without a chair, or walking with their feet tied, or grazing like Tityrus's stags in the air. They will take one view or another, but it will be a consistent view.'

To this extent, then, any fair reasoning—any reasoning, in fact, which proceeds honestly from the premisses, and does not keep one eye fixed all the time on a conclusion which it is predetermined to avoid—must lead to the admission that Cardinal Newman has proved his point, viz. that if we believe in infallible authority at all (and any authority to which we are bound to defer is practically and for us infallible authority), to Rome we must go in order to find it.

CHAPTER IV.

OUR next inquiry must be whether it follows still further from this that he has established the other horn of his dilemma, and proved also that there is no other alternative but that of Atheism; or, as he calls it, Liberalism. This I do not for a moment admit. As already suggested in the course of this paper, it appears to me that it is a mistake to view Cardinal Newman as a man who has passed through Protestantism to Anglicanism; and thence, finding both of them unsatisfactory, on, to find his ultimate rest in Rome. The truer account of him I take to be that he is a very devout and honest, as well as a very able man, but that he never was a Protestant at all. He had imbibed, or been taught, in his early years, dogmas which are held by Protestants, but he shows no trace of possessing what may be called a Protestant spirit; indeed, he does not seem even to understand it, and confounds it from the first with a merely sceptical, or, as he calls it, Liberal spirit. He has been, moreover, always a logician rather than a philosopher, and has appeared to care more for the consistency and cogency of his arguments, as arguments, than for the soundness of the premisses on which they are based. Thus it will be seen, on examining his position in the 'Apologia,' that he began with an abhorrence of what he calls Liberalism, and an assumption that authority must exist somewhere to withstand the solvent force of 'the wild living intellect of man.'

Starting from those assumptions, a logician could but arrive at the goal which he has reached, and the card castle of factitious Anglo-Catholicism would be but a trifling obstacle in his path; but to suppose that in overturning this he has any way struck at the root of genuine Protestant Christianity, is like supposing that a man who has demonstrated the futility of judicial astrology has thereby demolished scientific astronomy. Protestantism is a spirit rather than a form; indeed, many of the forms under which it appears and is judged are in fact little but old clothes borrowed from the ecclesiasticism which is its antithesis. The hard literalism of one sect, the shallow universalism of another, the rigid Calvinism of a third, are all instances of this. They seem to show only that when Christians escaped from the trammels of Rome in the sixteenth century there was still a marked tendency amongst them to fall back upon that over-dogmatic spirit which had itself led up by little and little to most of the Roman corruptions. And the spirit of Protestantism is exactly that spirit of liberty for which St. Paul contends so earnestly in the Epistle to the

Galatians, and elsewhere in his writings; and it is with this liberty, which he values so highly, that the whole spirit of sacerdotalism is bitterly, irreconcilably, and eternally at variance—a truth which was perceived by Luther in the very earliest days of the Reformation, even before the time of the Diet of Worms.[1]

This is the true ground upon which the battle at present raging in the Church of England has to be fought out, for this it is, far more than any particular dogma or any special ceremonial, which must determine finally whether in the future it is to continue Protestant or not. It is a common assumption in the present day, with Roman and semi-Roman controversialists alike, that when they have quoted the saying that 'the Bible and the Bible only is the religion of Protestants,' nothing more is required in order to demonstrate the absurdity of Protestantism. When it is honestly

---

[1] *D'Aubigné*, vol. ii. pp. 107-8, 3rd edit.

made it really demonstrates nothing except a confusion of thought on the part of the maker. It can but mean one of two things. Either it means to assert that modern criticism—historical, philological, and scientific—has so weakened the authority of the Bible, that it is an insufficient groundwork on which to found a religion, or else it means only what is self-evident enough, viz. that all sects, however incompatible their tenets may be, have professed to found them on the Bible.

Now, of these two significations, the first is an objection, not against Protestantism in particular, but against Christianity in general, and as such need not be discussed in this place. It is enough to remark that even if we adopt the extreme ecclesiastical view, and say that we accept not the Church on the authority of the Bible, but the Bible on the authority of the Church, still if the Bible is untrue the Church which affirms that it is true must itself be false, and the religion which is built upon the two must fall with them both. To persons discussing on first principles the truth of Christianity these questions are of importance, but as between different forms of professed Christianity they are entirely without significance. It can hardly be maintained, as it appears to me, by candid disputants, that the purgatory of criticism through which the Bible has been made to pass during the present century has on the whole weakened its position. The 'wood, hay, and stubble' of what has been well called bibliolatry—verbal inspiration, and ignorant, partial, ill-digested, and traditional interpretation—has indeed been burned, and the smoke of the conflagration has frightened many people into the belief that the whole edifice was being destroyed; but the foundation remains essentially uninjured by the fire. To drop metaphor, I cannot see that the results of criticism have been so formidable as some persons suppose, or that, with few and comparatively unimportant exceptions, an intelligent man is not as well entitled to believe that the books of the New Testament are the actual works of the authors to whom they are attributed, as that the bulk of the ancient classics are those of their accepted authors; or, again, that the Gospel history is as authentic as any other ancient history which we possess. The ultra-critical view, logically carried out, would question all history before the revival of learning, and might thus take an *à priori* objection to the possibility of any revelation of an older date than the invention of printing, not on philosophical but on historical grounds. Yet we can scarcely consent to believe that mankind had no history up to that date, or even that we know nothing of it.

It is the other objection, that taken from the various and contradictory conclusions which all profess to be derived from the Bible, with which alone we are here concerned. It is one which, like several other difficulties besetting subjects of no less importance to the welfare of mankind, does not admit of a formally complete answer; but it is far more formidable as a controversial weapon than as an obstacle to honest and earnest investigation. The objection might be included in the list of what Hooker [1] has called 'bug's words;' it is one, that is to say, which always carries with it a sort of *suggestio falsi*, and frightens people by begging the question in the act of stating it. It may be said then, that the differences of interpretation whic exist have certainly lost nothing in amount by the statements of adversaries; that they have been indefinitely multiplied and increased by the over-dogmatism of those who have invented them, and by whom the Bible has been constantly invoked to settle questions to which it has really no relation; that the Bible has been

[1] *Hooker*, Lib. I. vii. 6.

interpreted under the pressure of ignorance, prejudice, tradition, distortion by authority, often supported by force, and its interpretation thus encumbered by artificial difficulties which it is almost or quite impossible for any given age or any given individual entirely to shake off; and further, that the same differences existed to the full as much in primitive times, so called, as they do now.

Finally, it may be said in this case, as in the case above referred to of moral conduct, that man is placed in a position in which he must judge for himself, with imperfect data, but nevertheless on his own responsibility, and at his own risk; yet at the same time with a conviction that if he will but do his best in an honest and good heart, he will be enabled to find his way sufficiently for his own salvation; but he has to remember that God has given him reason to guide himself withal, and if he chooses not to use it, or to misapply it, he does so to his own cost. In the words of Bishop Jeremy Taylor, 'if a man will take my candle and hold it to the devil, he shall but burn his own fingers.' Finally, the infallible guide when we have got it seems to provide but a kind of 'infallibility limited.' Is it worth while to deny the evidence of reason, to swallow doctrines which contradict at once the evidence of the senses and the conscience, and the plainest words of Scripture, and to be left at last to take our choice between the morals of the Sermon on the Mount and the morals of the Probabilists?

Strangely enough, it is to a 'seventeenth century divine,' and one who owed his first advancement in the Church to Laud himself, that we have to go in order to get the arguments in favour of private judgment put with the greatest possible force. In Bishop Jeremy Taylor's treatise on 'Liberty of Prophesying' exactly the view here given is maintained, with all that vigour and learning which have made its author so justly famous. After showing in succession that tradition, councils, Popes, fathers, and the Church in general, all equally fail to establish a claim to be our infallible guide, he maintains that every man's reason must be his own guide, that he is bound to use the best help that he can from any or all of these sources, but not to follow any of them blindly, that he has the promise of God's own guidance, who will not punish him for errors which are not voluntary on his part. 'God,'[1] he says, 'will have no man pressed with another's inconveniences in matters spiritual and intellectual, no man's salvation to depend upon another; and every tooth that eats sour grapes shall be set on edge for itself, and for none else.'

[1] Taylor's works (Heber's edit.), vol. viii. p. 94. Taylor indeed in this work demolishes the argument from antiquity more completely, if possible, than even Cardinal Newman himself, showing that there exists no such thing as a 'consensus patrum,' and that S. Augustine, in particular, introduced doctrines 'which till his time no man preached.'—*Op. cit.*, p. 78.

Here, then, we arrive, by the aid of a Laudian divine, at the true principle of Protestantism, a principle which we all recognise as old enough, but which is and has been, whether recognised or not, an essential principle of Christianity from the time that our Lord said to the Jews 'why even *of yourselves* judge ye not what is right'— the Bible and private judgment. Every attempt to escape from this, whether in the region of belief or in that of morals, has led in all ages to the most monstrous results. 'By their fruits ye shall know them;' and the fruits of the principle of infallible authority, with its logical outcome in 'spiritual direction,' have led, as already suggested, in morals to Probabilism, and in theology to superstitions and idolatries contravening alike the words of Scripture and the reason of man.

CHAPTER V.

To those Englishmen who thought at all upon such matters for many generations anterior to the present, such statements as have just been made appeared as complete truisms as the proposition that liberty is better than slavery, or health to be preferred to sickness; it is therefore worth while in the next place to examine shortly what are the causes why, while we have been progressing with such rapidity in every other department of human thought and knowledge, we see in the present generation such an evident tendency to retrogression in the one matter of religious faith; and this not in one class only, but in several, and notably among the rich and fashionable. It is not too much to say that sixty years ago if an educated Englishman joined the Church of Rome, his doing so would have created more astonishment than would at this moment be excited by a similar person becoming a Mohammedan; and that if at the same date an English clergyman had ventured to preach the doctrine and practise the ritual which may be heard and seen in a hundred English churches next Sunday, he would have had no opportunity of repeating the offence; yet now all these things occur without exciting any surprise, and with scarcely more than a few murmurs of disapproval. To what causes are these vast changes due? and is the state of things which admits of them to be looked upon as an improvement or a deterioration—an advance or a retrogression?

We know well the stock answer of the partisan of the change, that it is due to increased zeal and learning on the part of the clergy, bringing once more into the light the almost forgotten claims of the Church to teach 'with authority,' and to the increased humility and teachableness of the laity, corresponding to and educed by this revival of clerical power, and concurring with it to produce the 'improved tone of Church feeling,' on which they are never tired of felicitating the existing generation. But a truer answer, if a less flattering one, would be to say that the causes are to be found in the increased wealth and luxury of the day, and in certain other characteristics—social, moral, and intellectual—more or less connected with this, either as causes or as effects, to wit idleness, cowardice, and religious indifference on the part of the laity; ambition, vanity, and poverty on that of the clergy: and appetite for excitement equally in both.

The greatest of all prevalent delusions, is the belief that the success of the High Church movement is any measure of the religious zeal of the day; it is, on the other hand, a very serious indication of the indifferentism of the lay Englishmen of the period. Englishmen, for generations past, when they have had any real care for religion at all, have been before all things Protestants; and so long as they remained really convinced Protestants, the one thing towards which they were a little inclined to be intolerant was that old hierarchical slavery which they believed their fathers had cast off for ever. They are, in feeling and disposition, much what they were, for national characteristics change but slowly; and it is just so far, and so far only, as they have unhappily acquired an indifference and a contempt for religion altogether,[1] that they are induced to admit hierarchical claims again in any degree, as believing that they are too unimportant to call for serious resistance.

It is true that this may not last for ever, that as a new generation rises up, mere use and custom may have habituated those who do not

[1] See, for example, *Bishop Thirlwall's Letters*, p. 380.

inquire for themselves to the recognition of clerical claims as in some way a matter of course; but it is no less the fact, that the existing English *père de famille* only does not resent them because he despises them, does not believe that they will ever come to anything; and since they and their various adjuncts amuse his idle daughters and give a harmless direction to the crude fancies of his foolish son, he is willing to endure them as he does the vagaries of 'high art,' and the eccentricities of juvenile politics; but he loves them none the better, and if he really cares for anything besides making money and advancing his own and his family's social position, he generally hates them pretty cordially.

Indifference is, and ever has been, acknowledged as the direct and natural fruit of increased wealth and luxury, and even those who fail at once to see the natural connection between the two, can hardly avoid observing the fact that luxurious living and High Churchism have been during the present generation advancing side by side, and may well ask with some uneasiness for an explanation of such a phenomenon. At any rate, it is observable that the two other periods when High Churchism found favour in England since the Reformation, were the reign of Charles I. and the reign of Charles II., and there are no two periods of our history of which from every point of view—moral, social, or political—we have more reason to be ashamed.

Again, idleness and cowardice are direct and admitted products of luxury, and they too in their turn tend directly to lead men to a sacerdotal religion. Idleness makes a man anxious to get his religion done for him by the parson, just as he gets his law business done for him by his solicitor, and his estate managed by his agent; and cowardice again pulls him in the same direction, by making him hate responsibility, and salve his conscience to the best of his ability by trying to shift off some of it on to the shoulders of the priest. Can we 'live for pleasure and lose nothing by it?' is the question which, consciously or unconsciously, a luxurious age sets before itself, and it is one which a sacerdotal religion and that alone seems to answer for a time at least in the affirmative. Such an answer must be a lie, for it is as contrary to the law of God as the transmutation of metals is to the law of nature; but as it ministers to human greed, it may sometimes be long before its falsehood becomes apparent. The discovery will come sooner or later, and the longer it is delayed, the more terrible will be its effects; but in the meantime, we need look no further to account for the favour which High Churchism notoriously finds among fashionable young ladies and dissipated young guardsmen, and the rich and luxurious classes generally.

There are, however, secondary causes to be

Romanism, Protestantism, Anglicanism. 91

found, which in a smaller way concur with these general ones. Not the smallest of these is the sensuous and theatrical character of the High Church services in their fullest development. People who have spent the week in rushing from one scene of dissipation to another, have no relish left for a simple service which requires for its appreciation some effort of the intellect and attention, some genuine and honest wish to lay the soul bare in the presence of its Maker, and, in the words of the poet, ' to sue, *in formâ pauperis*, to God.' Such persons naturally like something not quite so utterly opposed to all to which they devote themselves elsewhere, and go to what they are pleased to call a ' service,' which differs from the scenes of the week not much more than as an oratorio differs from an opera. A Sunday morning service in a fashionable church seems arranged on purpose to suggest the notion of a visit of ceremony to Almighty God, paid mainly with the view of showing how admirably

His worshippers have got on without Him during the week.

Sentimentality, sensuousness, self-indulgence—these are the characteristic products of the fag-end of the nineteenth century, shown in everything that we do, in our increased luxury and expensiveness of living, in our immensely multiplied holidays and amusements, in our enormous masses of light literature, in our increased devotion to what we call art and culture, and shown no less in our religious revival, which is turned in practice into little else than an additional form of luxury.

Such, then, being the influences which are at work upon the laity, let us now see whether there are not other special influences affecting the clergy, which, different though they be, are all tending to the production of similar general results.

That very great changes have been taking place in the position of the English clergy during the lifetime of the present generation there can be no doubt, and it seems only strange that they should not have attracted more general attention than they seem to have done, more especially as they all tend in the direction of transforming the English clergy into a class or caste more and more separate from other classes, and less and less like what they have been for generations past.

In the first place, their social position is changing. The times, which are witnessing an increased expenditure in all the classes around them, are bringing no increase of income, but a positive decrease, to them. Then the social changes in the country districts are affecting them in a similar way. The class of smaller and moderate living squires is rapidly disappearing, and the place of half a dozen such is now commonly occupied by the estate of some *parvenu* millionaire, who is rarely at his country house, and with whom the parson cannot associate on equal terms, when he is; and in consequence the latter, unless he cares to hob and nob with his farmer neighbours, has scarcely any other associates than his clerical brethren around.

Again, clerical education is also changing. Partly in consequence of the social and economical facts just noticed, partly of the general pressure upwards from below affecting the clerical as well as other professions, a far smaller proportion of the clergy than was formerly the case receive their education at the Universities of Oxford and Cambridge, and the institution of theological colleges, so called, in some degree a consequence of this, tends still further to diminish it.

Once more, the secularisation of the Universities has produced a great effect in the same direction, and will produce yet more. I am not here discussing whether this was right or wrong, necessary or unnecessary: what I say is, that whereas twenty years ago there were in

Oxford alone some 450 fellowships, of which in round numbers 300 were held by clerics, and most of the rest by persons about to become such, there are now scarcely more than 100 clerical fellows in the whole University, and the number is still diminishing. A similar state of things exists also, I believe, at Cambridge; and one result of it is, that whereas a very large proportion of the honour men of the Universities previously to that time took Holy Orders, now the clerical profession, or that part of it which is educated at the Universities at all, is supplied to a large extent from the dregs of the pass-men, and the effect of this is beginning already to extend to the country at large. College livings, which were formerly always held by ex-fellows, are now constantly given away elsewhere, and not a few of the advowsons sold; and although a college incumbent was by no means always looked upon as a model 'parish priest' (as it is now the fashion to call a parochial minister), yet he was generally a kind of intellectual aristocrat among his neighbours, and often a man far less narrow and professional in his sympathies than they.

All these causes then, aided perhaps by the increased opportunities afforded to men of intelligence and education of getting into Government employ, in India and elsewhere, are concurring to bring about a great alteration in the personal characteristics as well as in the status of the English clergy. They are gradually losing the influence derived from social position and wealth and education, and they are at the same time drawing more and more together, becoming more and more professional. It is no wonder then if they are tempted to try and make the latter change compensate for the former. Influence is a necessity of their position; and if they are losing that which they had as Christian gentlemen and scholars, the readiest mode of recovering it is to endeavour to make themselves priests. Such influence is of a lower and ignobler kind, but by no means therefore the less powerful.

Mankind may be roughly divided into those who are susceptible to religious motives and those who are not; and if the former division, which is by far the larger, can once be got to look upon the clergyman as the priest, who in some sense differs from other men, and possesses, as they do not, the keys of the kingdom of Heaven, there is no fear that his influence will be slight. Amongst the unthinking portion of mankind, whether belonging to the classes conventionally called ignorant or not, a strong tendency always exists to put superstition and something scarcely distinguishable from magic in the place of religion, to trust in a greater or less degree in rites and ceremonies and forms of words, and this above all in the hour of death and amid the terrors which belong to such a time. Men seem to long for something which shall save them without any labour of their own, and which being mysterious and unintelligible they can accept without the trouble of inquiring into its credentials, and with a kind of half-acknowledged idea that it will serve them as a valid excuse that they knew no better—even though they took no pains to know. That this condition of mind has not become extinct in the midst of the enlightenment of the nineteenth century, let the success of mesmerism and homœopathy and spiritualism suffice to witness: and such a condition of mind affords a well-prepared seed-bed for a sacerdotal religion.

Thus we see, even in this imperfect and hurried view, how many circumstances concur to adapt both the laity and clergy at the present time for a great retrogressive reaction in the direction of a priestly religion.

It would be wrong, however, to suppose that the clergy are as a rule at all conscious agents in the mischief which they are doing. Men

Romanism, Protestantism, Anglicanism. 99

believe readily what it is their wish or their interest to believe, and the more so when they have been by previous instruction carefully prepared and trained to believe it; and a large portion of the younger clergy of the present day, while as we have seen less well educated, less intelligent, and less widely cultured than their predecessors, have had more of actual theological training, and that mostly of a one-sided kind. I would not willingly calumniate or misrepresent them. They are, I believe, no worse either morally or intellectually than the rank and file of any other profession not better paid or better looked on than their own, but they are also ceasing to be better than these, because, from the causes already mentioned, their position is becoming worse; and consequently, like these, they are, as they grow more professional, growing also more subject to the defects especially incident to their own particular profession. And being trained up now to a belief in all the same claims and powers which are asserted for the Roman priesthood, and which fifty years since were undreamed of by the English clergy, they put them forward with perfect good faith, and often with a not unnatural eagerness to make the most of them, and become themselves the principal agents in the reaction of the time.

That the only logical, or, in plain English, the only reasonable end of this reaction must be re-union with Rome, it has been the business of the earlier part of this paper, with the help of Cardinal Newman, to show. It is not too much to say that every argument which can be used against submission to Rome tells with tenfold greater force against submission to the claims of modern High Anglicanism, while those in use against Protestantism retain all their validity as against the English Church.

A striking confirmation of the view here maintained has been brought to my notice since it was written in a passage from the 'Life of the late Bishop Wilberforce' (vol. ii. pp. 49-50), in which the following account is given of the reason which induced Archdeacon (now Cardinal) Manning to join the Church of Rome. The editor says, 'he believed that what he had supposed to be the theology of the English Church was only the opinion of a school, *beginning with the end of Queen Elizabeth's reign*, and neutralised at the Revolution.' Here is accurately given, in a single sentence, the true historical account of the genesis of High Churchism in the English Church; and the questions which it raises are these two: How is it possible upon any sort of legitimate Church theory that a body, which had been entirely Protestant for almost fifty years, which though it had retained bishops had retained them merely as officials, which had broken away from the sacramental theory of the whole Western Church of the time, and which admitted non-episcopal orders; by the action, not of the whole body, but of a mere party within it, should reassume all these doctrines and functions as if it had maintained them throughout, and should assert a claim to authority different from, repudiated by, and utterly repugnant to that of the body from which it had broken off, and yet professing to be derived only from the old stock from which it could not and does not attempt to deny that that other body is legitimately descended? And again, How is it possible for such a body to assert successfully such a position, when the stem from which it is separated, and whose legitimacy it does not attempt to impugn, has expressly cut it off from the Church by a solemn anathema never since removed?[1]

The position of the Anglican Church upon the Catholic theory is a hopeless one. It cannot deny the catholicity of the Roman Church, the legitimacy of its succession, or the validity of its ordinances; but in allowing these it em-

[1] See Rev. T. Mozley's *Reminiscences*, vol. ii. p. 332.

phatically condemns itself, inasmuch as the Roman Church—thus Catholic and legitimate—anathematises it. From this dilemma there is no escape. If Rome is not heretical, Anglicanism must be schismatic. But the dilemma is the creation of the High Church and anti-Protestant party alone; for while Anglicans held that the Pope was Antichrist and the Church of Rome the synagogue of Satan, it was clear that the anathemas of such a body mattered nothing to them. But we did not then try 'to run with the hare and hunt with the hounds.'

We may then finally conclude that while Cardinal Newman has shown conclusively enough that the principle of authority can lead to nothing else than submission to Rome, he has quite failed to establish the other horn of his dilemma; for he has not shown either that the authority of Rome itself is incontrovertible, or that the principle of private judgment leads to atheism. Rather, on the other hand, the argument from analogy which he himself invokes seems to point to the conclusion that mankind can look for no infallible authority. And if we accept the test commended to us in the Gospel itself—' by their fruits ye shall know them,'—bad as the Protestant world may be, he must be a bold man who will maintain that the Romish world is better.

CHAPTER VI.

THERE are some few other thoughts which the foregoing considerations, together with the actual phenomena of the religious reaction going on about them and among them, should force upon the minds of all Englishmen who believe in Christian truth, who love their country, and who would not willingly see it sink into that most hopeless of all conditions, in which religion—officially so called—is enlisted on one side, and all the intelligence and honesty of the nation on the other. It is impossible not to see that the ablest and most honest minds amongst the High Church clergy have joined the Church of Rome, from Newman and Manning and the Wilberforces down to those many less illustrious persons whose secessions are from time to time reported in the papers of the day. Almost every leader of the early stage of the Oxford movement sooner or later did so, except the few whose minds were steadied by the artificial ballast of the possession of dignities and rich preferments. Some of them were men, as Montalembert truly said of them, 'of whom the world was not worthy,' who gave up all that makes life dear to follow their honest convictions.

Again, it is almost impossible not to see that the movement, in its more modern and so-called Ritualistic form, has lost everything that once made it worthy of honour. Writers such as I have quoted above—Newman on the one hand, Lightfoot on the other—have shown conclusively that its claims have no foundation either in logic or in history. Its tendency in the direction of Rome, always suspected by its opponents and always denied by its partisans, has become more and more unmistakable, and indeed it is likely to be far less harmful when it does lead to Rome than when, irrationally and unwarrantably as we have seen, it stops short of it: for it is now quite clear that the Ritualistic clergy are endeavouring to re-establish one by one all the superstitions and abominations which were cast off at the Reformation.

We find now in churches belonging to the National Church many of the practices and almost all the doctrines the absence of which for three hundred years has distinguished the Reformed Churches from Rome—auricular confession, the Mass, images and pictures of the blessed Virgin; in a word, all that is implied in or connected with sacerdotalism in its most extravagant form, always with the one important exception of the acknowledgment of the authority of the Pope. And this one exception affords indeed in very many cases the key to the whole position, for the Ritualistic clergy are in point of fact mere anarchists. Their position in matters ecclesiastical is strictly comparable to that of the Irish Land Leaguers in matters political; for under the pretence of objecting to what they please to call usurped authority, they practically acknowledge no authority at all : they refuse obedience to the law of the land as soon as it comes into conflict with their own opinions, and in like manner limit their obedience to the Bishop at the precise point at which episcopal admonitions cease to be agreeable to them.

Posing in the first instance as the supporters of 'authority' and impugners of 'private judgment,' it has now become evident that the only authority to which they are themselves prepared to defer is their own, and the private judgment to which they object is that of everybody except themselves. Thus professing to be before all men catholic and orthodox, the ground which they occupy is exactly that of the most lawless heretics—indeed, the very word heresy ($αἵρεσις$, free choice) exactly expresses their position. If any one doubts this let him compare the mode in which Cardinal Newman speaks of the authority of his (Anglican) Bishop and of the obedience which he paid him, in the 'Apologia,' with the utterances of the Ritualistic clergy in regard to their own diocesans. And this is a matter of more importance than may at first appear, for, as has been well remarked, it is just the admirable discipline and strict subordination in which the Romish clergy have been kept which has alone rendered their pretensions endurable by civilised men, and they have often been found but barely endurable; and if the Anglican clergy are to be permitted to assert all the same claims, and at the same time to renounce all discipline as they are now doing, they will in the course of a very few years bring about a state of things which will be quite unendurable. Disciplined troops are bad enough, but deliver us above all things from *francs tireurs*.

The final conclusion, deducible equally from reason and from history, seems to be that of the three kinds of Christianity which we have considered Romanism and Protestantism are clearly contradictory, irreconcilable, mutually destructive. Romanism—once grant its primary assumption of the need for and existence of some one plenary infallible authority to which mankind is bound to defer, seems to fulfil in theory, and if we may believe many of its recent converts, can also fulfil in practice, all its promises—can, when its action is not interfered with, still every doubt, command every passion, every affection, every thought. But though this may be true in individual cases, the state of the Catholic world scarcely commends it to us in the gross—and then its primary assumption *is* an assumption. It rests on no sufficient evidence from history, and contradicts the whole analogy of nature, besides always suggesting the doubt, in the cases of those not born to it, whether, after all, the system has really relieved them of their individual responsibility, or whether, on the other hand, the act of choosing it does not involve individual responsibility for all that follows.

Protestantism also starts with an assumption, but its only necessary assumption is that of the general truth of the New Testament history; and the evidence for this would appear to be as good as that for any other ancient history we have. With this for a ground-plan man is left to guide himself by the aid of that 'Light which lighteth every man that cometh into the world'—call it reason, call it conscience, moral sense, or by what name you please—and this is strictly in accordance with the analogy of nature. As in morals a man can have a general rule of right and wrong but not an infallible guide in individual cases, and as he may err by laxity on the one side or over-scrupulousness on the other; and as in ordinary affairs of life a similar rule holds good, and prudence is the golden mean between carelessness and over-caution,—so, in matters of faith a man may rationalise himself into believing nothing, or carry his faith to the excesses of a paltry and frivolous superstition; but he may also in the one case, as in the other, hold the balance fairly even, and he will in the one case, as in the other, assuredly suffer in proportion as he fails so to do.

The great principle of Protestantism is that, having assured mankind, as every Christian system must do, in name at least, of a Saviour who is Himself the God-man, it admits of none besides, and allows no shadow of human authority to intervene between Him and the individual human soul. To it the idea of a priesthood, in any proper sense of the word, is not only unchristian, but is distinctively anti-christian.

What, then, is Anglicanism, of which we hear

so much? and where is it to be found? It cannot be, as so many people seem to fancy it, something between these two, else it would be, in Dr. Newman's words quoted above, 'holding a balance between opposites so skilfully as to do without fulcrum or beam.' It was for the first century of its existence, and has been mainly since, what most persons up to forty or fifty years ago would have called it, simply a form of Protestantism peculiar to England. So long as it remains so, it occupies a position in the ecclesiastical order not unlike that of constitutional monarchy in the political order; essentially Protestant, though wearing the form of ancient Catholicism, as the latter is essentially democratic, though in the guise of monarchy. But when it begins to call itself Catholic, and to revive the claims of an authoritative priesthood to the obedience of men, it is compelled at once to break with logic and to falsify history; and its acceptance, so far as it is accepted by intelligent and honest minds, is a measure simply of their ignorance of the one or their incapacity for the other, or else of an easy credulity equally indifferent to both.

There is one special form of criticism to which much of what I have now written is likely to be exposed, which I am anxious to meet by anticipation. I shall no doubt be charged with uncharitableness, and be told that in attacking as I have done the position of a particular party in the Church, I have, in fact, assailed a number of the most laborious and devoted men at present to be found within her bounds. This is a species of criticism which is always easy, and which, especially with kindly disposed and not very well-informed or thoughtful persons, is apt to carry far more weight than really belongs to it. It is not true that to attack the principles of a party, whether religious or political, is to attack the characters of the individuals who compose it. That is the general answer to such a charge.

But, moreover, the accusation is too general to be really effective. No movement could ever rise into importance unless it recommended itself to some minds of superior power, to some zealous and self-devoted souls; and the Oxford movement of 1833 was singularly favoured in these respects. And again, when once any movement has so far succeeded as to become one of the leading influences in its day, it follows of necessity that it attracts into itself a vast proportion of such excellent persons; for, as time goes on, it becomes in many cases the first powerful influence to which their minds are subjected in those years of youth and early manhood which so often give the permanent direction to their future activity. But, especially in the case of religious movements, the most devout, the most zealous, even the most influential minds are not always the most learned, the most impartial, or the most capable of accurately weighing evidence; and hence the fact, if it be a fact, that at any particular time even the greater number of pious and devoted men are to be found in the ranks of a particular party is no proof that the principles of that party are true, or the reasoning upon which they are founded legitimate. Were it otherwise there could be no such thing as truth or falsehood in reasoning at all; for, to take the instance most germane to our subject, what may be said of the High Church party in the present day might have been said with even greater truth of the Evangelical party at the beginning of the present century, which at that time appeared to most observers to have a positive monopoly of whatever piety and zeal existed in the English Church.

I disclaim, therefore, in the strongest terms any intention to undervalue the zeal, devotion, and unselfishness which are to be found in large measure amongst the High Church party, though at the same time I believe that it owes some portion of its present success, as all successful parties do, to the fact that it harmonises with and fosters some of those tastes and foibles which belong to the age irrespectively of its religion, and which in themselves are neither religious nor in any way admirable.

CHAPTER VII.

THE foregoing essay had been completed before I had become acquainted with Dr. Littledale's now well-known work—'Plain Reasons against Joining the Church of Rome.' It might seem, perhaps, at first, that there is no special reason why I should notice in this place a book which is a mere anti-Roman polemic, containing but little that is new. I do so, however, because from the well-known position of the author, who has gained a reputation as a kind of lanzknecht of the extreme Anglican party, it must be evident that he occupies exactly the ground which in the above pages I have been at some pains to prove to be untenable.

I will first observe that the writings of Dr.

Littledale, and especially the little book in question, appear to constitute a kind of new departure on the part of the faction to which he belongs, which must, one would suppose, be in the highest degree distasteful to its older and more decorous members; for while they almost, from the first rise of the Oxford movement, have treated the Roman Church with respect and even veneration, though differing from her, he, on the other hand, has not scrupled to bespatter her with a shower of λοιδορία, not unlike that with which he has elsewhere overwhelmed the Protestant Reformers. And this new departure is not altogether unimportant, for it seems to show one of two things, either that the party thus making it feels, or fancies it feels, its own strength, like the young German Empire, and hence intends to make good its pretensions equally against Rome and Protestantism, the France and Russia which encroach upon it; or else that it really feels its own weakness, that it is seriously alarmed, as it well may be, at the number of desertions from its ranks to those of Rome, and is therefore making a public and violent demonstration against Rome, in the hope of persuading the English public that there is nothing Romanising in its own principles or tendencies. Perhaps both these feelings may exist in different degrees in various members of the party.

Turning now to the work itself, the first point which will strike any reader at all familiar with anti-Roman polemics of older date will probably be—what I must be excused for calling—the extremely stale character of the facts and arguments made use of. There is a sense, indeed, in which this is natural and inevitable ; the controversy between Romanism and Protestantism has lasted upwards of three centuries and a half. In the first half-century of its existence it engaged all the energies of men at the least as acute and learned as any who have followed them, and it would be strange indeed if these men, working under the stimulus of the strongest of worldly motives—often having their own lives at stake—over and above those which they had in common with their successors, had not placed in the fullest light all the facts and arguments which could be found in their time; and but few of first-rate importance have been added since. But it is not obvious, unless for the reason already suggested, why a gentleman chiefly famous hitherto for flaying Protestants, should feel suddenly inspired to collect together all this good old Protestant thunder, and hurl it at the head of the Pope for the edification of the English nation. No person not a Roman Catholic need object to the special points which Dr. Littledale makes against Rome—the charges which he brings on the score of mariolatry, of image worship, of dishonest dealing with the Decalogue, of discouraging the study of Scripture, and the like; and, above all, of setting up, by her support of the Jesuit and other casuists, a vicious and antichristian code of morals, leading directly to the very results with which our Lord reproached the Pharisees. With all this I am not concerned—further than to remark, as I have already done, that it is exactly the old stock-in-trade of Protestant argument against Rome, and in no way peculiar to Dr. Littledale and his school. What is peculiar to him, and what I am specially concerned to deal with, is, firstly, that what he omits to say is far more important and characteristic than what he says; and, secondly, that if we leave facts and go to principles, it will be found that every principle which he invokes tells against himself with at least as much force as against Rome.

Thus, though he dilates much upon the subjects above mentioned, and many others like them, he appears to include sacerdotalism and the doctrine of the Eucharist in his list of 'matters of which it can fairly be said that Rome and England have common ground of agreement, however they may differ in detail or in mode of expression.'[1]

Now, of these two doctrines it may be safely stated that while the latter has been from the beginning the main point in dispute between Roman and Protestant Christians, and especially between Rome and England, the former bears the same relation both to it and all these other points which the root does to the stem and branches of a tree—it was the starting-point and origin of them all. There could be no priesthood if there were not mysterious rites and privileges of which the priests alone possessed the key, nor could such rites long maintain their mystic character without a priesthood interested in maintaining it. Thus these two doctrines are correlative to each other, and they it is which constitute the core and essence of Roman Catholic religion; the others

[1] See *Prefatory Note.*

being merely the leaves, buds, and fruits of the tree, of which these two form the root and stem.

Coming now to principles, Dr. Littledale starts [1] with affirming two sources from which we are to judge of any doctrine submitted to us, viz. the Bible and Church history, and he states the relations of these two authorities to each other with a degree of appositeness which deserves to be noted. He says: [2] 'Whenever we hold any doctrine which is found alike in the Bible and in the teaching of the Christian Church ever since, we can be quite certain that here is an integral piece of the original Christian religion. But if we cannot find it in the Bible at all, nor in Church history, for a very long time, then the evidence is all against it; and there is very great unlikelihood of its being part of the Gospel revelation. For the broad rule is, that while the antiquity of a doctrine does not prove its *truth*,

[1] P. 15.   [2] P. 16.

since it may be a mere survival from one of the early heretical sects ; yet its *novelty* proves its *falsehood,* in not being part of the original and unchangeable revelation of God. When we can lay our finger on any particular tenet or practice, and say, " Up to such and such a date this was unknown to Christians, and did not come in till afterwards," we have disproved its claim to be part of the primitive faith, just as we should disprove the genuineness of a panel picture declared to be three or four hundred years old, if we showed it to be painted on mahogany, a wood which did not come into practical use till about 1720.'

In subsequent passages, where the exigencies of his argument against specific Roman doctrines or practices appear to require it, we find these principles further developed and explained ; *e.g.* when, in speaking of the express condemnation by some of the fathers of the use of images, he continues, ' Without mentioning those *whose entire silence implies their ignorance* of any such use.'[1] And again, the whole section entitled 'The Fathers on Bible Reading'[2] consists of a string of quotations from those authorities in condemnation of any doctrine not to be found in the Scriptures; and, in fact also, not to be so found by the use of reason or private judgment—as, for instance, the following passage from S. Basil: 'For practical purposes it is useful and necessary that *every one* should thoroughly learn out of the divinely inspired Scriptures, both for the fulfilment of piety, *and also in order not to become habituated to human traditions.*'[3]

Again, in dealing with the subject of 'Roman Untrustworthiness,' Dr. Littledale has occasion to refer to the innumerable forgeries and falsifications of decrees of councils, treatises of fathers, &c., which became so common in the Middle

---

[1] P. 42. [2] Pp. 94–7.
[3] Pp. 113 *et seq.*

Ages; and in so doing he points out, as the earliest instance, an attempt on the part of the Pope in the year 419 to palm off upon a council at Carthage a forged canon of the first General Council—an attempt deliberately repeated thirty years later by no less a person than S. Leo the Great; and in the section so entitled he accepts private judgment as fully as would the extremest ultra-Protestant; and he further quotes some very sweeping anti-Roman principles from the well-known Jesuit writer, Véron, of which the following are two: (1) No doctrine delivered since the time of the apostles can be an article of the Faith, even if confirmed by miracles;[1] (2) Nothing can be an article of the Faith which is grounded on texts which have been diversely interpreted by the fathers, or by approved theologians of later date.[2]

Now these principles fairly applied lead directly, necessarily, immediately, to the old

[1] P. 129. [2] P 195.

Protestant theory stated above, that nothing is to be considered of the essence of Christianity but that which is to be found in the Bible; and that of what is to be found in the Bible each man must judge for himself with the best means which he has at his disposal, and at his own proper risk. This is so plainly expressed in the passages just referred to, that it would be a bad compliment to the reader's intelligence to draw it from them in words. They are fatal to Romanism—no one doubts it; but assuredly to High Anglicanism they are more fatal still. You may not find Invocation or the Primacy of S. Peter in the Bible, but neither will you find the Apostolical Succession or Auricular Confession, or the doctrine of the Mass; or any of those wondrous practices and ceremonies which have sometimes led ill-instructed Roman Catholics to mistake a Ritualistic Church for one belonging to their own communion, and which Dr. Littledale so complacently and unaccountably disavows in the last page of his book. There is nothing but antiquity to fall back upon ; and antiquity, as we have seen already, with the help of Cardinal Newman, breaks down under the demand made upon it. How should it do otherwise? since the record is not only imperfect, but has been from almost the earliest times encumbered with uncertainties, and complicated with forgeries and falsifications innumerable.

Some of Dr. Littledale's principles are even too sweeping not only for his own theory, but for almost all known forms of Christianity; since it is pre-eminently true of the Nicene Creed itself, that we can 'put our finger upon it, and say up to such and such a date (viz., in this case 325) this was unknown to Christians,'[1] &c. And herein lies the truth of the statement that Dr. Littledale's arguments tell with more force against the High Anglican than even against the Roman position. As soon as you leave

[1] P. 15.

the New Testament, and get to ecclesiastical history, you lose all intelligible ground on which to draw a line between what is to be accepted as authoritative and what is not, unless you accept the Roman Church as the Church, and look upon all who differ from it as heretics.

A Protestant accepts the Nicene Creed because he believes it agrees with the Bible—a Romanist, because it is part of the credenda of the Church; and on the same grounds, *mutatis mutandis*, the one rejects and the other accepts the doctrine of the Immaculate Conception. But a High Anglican has no fixed ground at all. If he goes by antiquity, he can only go by the opinions of the majority for the time being; and had he lived in the middle of the fifth century, he would have had to be an Eutychian, in the short interval between the Robber Synod and the Council of Chalcedon.

If the Reformation be looked upon as a distinct assertion of the principle of private judgment, *as against* that of Church authority, there is solid ground for such an opinion. But on any other view it is not easy to make good a defence against the Roman argument that there is no difference between the Reformation and any of the previous schisms which had occurred between the separation of East and West and the sixteenth century, such as that of the Berengarians, the Albigenses, or the Lollards, except that it was on a larger scale and more successful. Several of these broke away from the Church on the very same grounds as the Reformers of the sixteenth century; viz., those of the sacerdotal power and the doctrine of the Mass. With regard to all these alike a Roman Catholic may say, 'The Church has always remained the Church. All these, and countless other heretical sects, have broken off from her, and been cast forth like a branch and withered; but nobody, except themselves, has ever doubted which was the Church and which the sect. Precisely the same thing happened in the sixteenth century, only on a larger scale. Why should that make so much difference?'

The answer of the Anglican controversialists of late years has been to admit the whole indictment as regards the foreign Protestant churches, but to meet it in their own case by an endeavour to make the Anglican Church what they consider Catholic, as one may say, in spite of itself. This, indeed, was the whole point of the famous Tract Ninety, and of sundry defences of the Anglican Ordinal from the High Church point of view; and is, in fact, nothing else but an ultra-legal—I had almost said a pettifogging—mode of argument, which serves to show to what shifts their authors have been driven, but does not reflect much credit upon their advocacy nor afford much real support to their cause. In substance, it amounts to this—that the English Reformers who compiled the Liturgy and drew up the Articles had all the will in the world to make them anti-Catholic, but that being constrained in some sort to keep up appearances, they have in fact failed in their object, and have left in them words enough to carry, by a little judicious manipulation, a so-called Catholic sense, and consequent efficacy from a Catholic point of view. This is applying to sacred and most important subjects a mode of proceeding with which we are all only too familiar in its application to Acts of Parliament, and which even in their case is frequently and not always unfairly denounced as a scandalous abuse of ingenuity. In the present instance, it may fairly be placed in the same category with those devices of the Jesuit casuists, on which Dr. Littledale is so justly severe. But in regard to the probability that the writers in question did actually fail in their intention, a recent

Catholic writer has very well pointed out,[1] firstly, that the fact that they had themselves been Catholic priests, and therefore well knew the intention of Catholic forms, gives a force to mere omissions in their case which would hardly belong to them in the writings of other men; and secondly, that 'the obvious fact that the Reformers could have had no serious objection to the retention of the ancient Catholic form, save that they did not approve its sense, is surely good evidence that they did not replace it by a form which bore that same sense.'[2]

These last arguments, if fairly weighed, will, I think, be admitted to have no little force. The High Church clergy now contend that they possess the whole powers of the Catholic priesthood in the fullest sense—that they are in fact sacrificing priests—and this in virtue of that which accordance with Catholic theory

---

[1] A. W. Hutton, *The Anglican Ministry*, p. 92.
[2] *Ibid.* p. 157.

alone can give them, viz. unbroken descent from the apostles, in a line of duly ordained persons; and this Dr. Littledale clearly implies throughout his book, both by his statements and his omissions. Now admitting as being at least doubtful, and for the sake of avoiding an elaborate historical argument, that they can make out an ecclesiastical pedigree without a break in the line of *persons ordained*, let us look for a moment at the chief points in the evidence as to the other requirement, viz. that the persons so ordained should have been *duly and adequately ordained* to enable them to possess and transmit the vast powers thus claimed for them.

The Reformation was, before all things, a great revolt against sacerdotalism. In a very early stage of it—viz., in 1520—Luther wrote, in the same address already referred to [1]:—' If any pious laymen were banished to a desert island,

[1] See above, p. 75.

and, having no regularly consecrated priest among them, were to agree to choose for that office one of their number, married or unmarried, this man would be as truly a priest as if he had been consecrated by all the bishops in the world.'[1] Indeed, as the Reformers—German, Swiss, and English—one and all denied in the strongest terms that there is any sacrifice in the Eucharist for a priest to offer, they could hardly have done other than deny the existence of a priest to offer it. Of the doctrines held by the compilers of the English Liturgy individually there is no doubt. They were among the most learned men of a learned age, they had themselves been Catholic priests in a time of controversy, and knew thoroughly well the intention and the implication of all the words and forms contained in the Roman Ordinal. If, then, such men, under such circumstances, altered these words and forms, there can be no reason-

[1] *D'Aubigné*, vol. ii. p. 108.

able doubt but that they altered the sense also, unless they were unable to express their own meaning in words.

When we add to this, that for the first hundred years after the words were altered no one ever doubted but that the sense was altered too, the case becomes almost too plain for argument. But even yet it is not half stated—for if we could suppose, notwithstanding all this, that no essential alteration was effected in the words of the Ordinal, what would it avail? The rest of the Church, the ancient body from which the Anglicans had broken off, and which always had and has a 'living voice,' did not acknowledge the 'orders' conferred by these forms, but always held them as null and void; and does so still. True it is that a curious and doubtful antiquarianism has raked up a few questionable cases, in which an individual Roman priest or a nationalist Gallican bishop is believed to have recognised Anglican orders as valid, but the judgment of the Roman Church, as a whole, has been and is unequivocally against them.

And there is a stronger point still—if this were not enough. What is known as the doctrine of 'intention'—that is to say, the belief that unless a priest in the performance of his functions intends, at least in a general way, to do that which the Church proposes as the purpose of the ordinance, then the ordinance itself is void—is, as we all know, repudiated by the High Anglicans as an innovation introduced by the Council of Trent; and whatever may be the general merits of the question, they clearly gain vastly by its rejection, as regards the point now in question, for otherwise it is evident enough that their claim to any sort of succession could not be maintained. Nevertheless, the alternative resulting from it is hardly all which we might suppose them to desire; for in order to maintain the validity of Anglican orders, it seems necessary to believe that bishops who had no thought of conveying sacerdotal powers to the deacons whom they ordained, must nevertheless have done so, and this by the use of a form of ordination from which all efficacy for that purpose was believed to have been designedly eliminated, and when the deacons so made priests had equally little intention of receiving any such powers, which they would have rejected as a blasphemous imposture.

Let him believe all this who can, but let him who does so remember that if it were true, it would reduce the whole theory of the priesthood to a level with such stories as that which the Laureate tells in the 'Idylls of the King,' where Vivien, by merely repeating a form of spell which she does not understand, brings upon Merlin a trance, from which neither she nor wiser than she is able to awake him. This is really no exaggeration. Cranmer and his fellows altered the form of ordination on purpose to exclude the hypothesis of conveying sacerdotal powers—though it is argued, on fine drawn antiquarian grounds, that they did not succeed quite as completely as they intended to do and believed they did. Coverdale and Parker, Grindal and Jewell, and other Edwardine and Elizabethan bishops, would have died before they would have ordained—even if they could have done so—a sacrificing priest; nor would the recipients of orders at their hands for a moment have consented to be made such; and this state of things continued, with the short and terrible interlude of Mary's reign, from 1552, when Edward's Ordinal came into use, till 1662, when the additions still used were inserted; so that even if these additions had constituted a valid form of ordination—which Roman Catholic writers persistently deny—yet the succession would have been broken beyond the possibility of recovery.

But of all these objections Dr. Littledale

candidly disposes in a single parenthesis, as 'cavils about the Ordinal'!!

It is in a similar spirit of mingled antiquarianism and quibbling that he endeavours at the same time to explain away the fact that the English Church was for centuries quite indistinguishable from the Roman, and to suggest, rather than assert, that its orders were derived from a separate source from those of Rome. He tells us [1] that 'only a very small part of the work of Christianising England was really effected by St. Augustine's mission, and by far the larger part of the conversion of Saxon England was achieved by the non-Roman missionaries of the Scoto-Irish Church;' and then alleges some purely technical grounds for disputing the fact that the English Church had ever in fact submitted to Rome.[2] Now these propositions may be capable of some sort of support by special pleading, or they may not. The

[1] P. 209. [2] P. 216.

former of them seems about as profitable a speculation as would be the discussion of the exact proportion of British, Roman, Saxon, Danish, and Norman blood to be found in any particular class of Englishmen, say in the sixteenth century. The latter is so technical, so much in fact the objection of an advocate raising quibbling points of law for lack of any rational or equitable plea in favour of his client, that it is difficult to treat it seriously. The objections [1] are that the Pope could not accept the submission of a foreign church without violating his coronation oath, that such submission could only be made by the bishops, if authorised by a national synod, which was never done; and that even if it had been its acts would have been void, because founded upon a belief in the genuineness of the famous false decretals.

All this may sound very plausible, but it is obvious that exactly the same might be said of

---

[1] Dr. Littledale states these in the reverse order.

the Church in France, Spain, Germany, or Italy itself. Such reasoning is, in fact, an evasion of the point at issue. The rise of the Papal power as such is a separate question not applying directly to the present case. The state of facts which it is intended to meet is quite a different one, viz. this, not so much that there was a Church of England subject to the Pope, as that from, at any rate, the Norman Conquest downwards, there was no Church of England distinguishable from the Church of Rome in any sense which was not equally applicable to the Church in France or elsewhere. The English Church had become as completely one with the rest of the Western Church as the Danes and Normans had become one with the English nation; and the attempt to reassert the independence of the English Church in the sixteenth century is about as hopeful and as rational as to assert the independent rights of kingdoms of the Heptarchy at the same time. It would be a very similar proceeding to argue from the history of Israel after the separation of the ten tribes that the Churches of Judah and Israel never had been one, and to support the view by a reference to the stories which show the comparative independence of the different tribes in the times of the Judges.

As with the question of sacerdotalism, so also with the doctrine of the Eucharist. Dr. Littledale does not discuss it except in relation to some comparatively unimportant points, such as the Roman refusal of the cup to the laity, implying thereby, in accordance with the passage already cited,[1] that the two Churches are at one in regard to it, an hypothesis which the whole history of the Reformation contradicts.

It appears needless to pursue the subject further. The reader who has followed me thus far will not have failed to perceive that Dr. Littledale's book, so far from making good the

[1] P. 80.

High Anglican position, merely affords an additional proof of its untenableness. He has saved appearances, it is true, by the simple, but not very candid, device of leaving out of view the main points of the Anglican position as against Rome, and directing attacks, 'full of sound and fury,' against a number of comparatively unimportant outworks; but in so doing he has constantly occupied ground untenable except upon the principles of that very Protestantism which he has so constantly reprobated, and which in its turn would entirely repudiate him and all his works. He appears to have calculated largely on the ignorance or idleness of his readers, in believing that they would take for granted his enumeration of the errors of Rome, and be too ill-informed or too careless to perceive that he had omitted the most fundamental and important of them. It may be hoped, however, that not a few among the number of readers whom he appears to have secured may be sufficiently informed, and sufficiently in earnest, to discover this for themselves. Thus he may lead some at last to see that if High Anglicanism be not merely the halfway-house to Rome, it must be the very newest and most lawless of dissenting sects—successful for the moment, because happening to fall in with, and to pander to some of, the characteristic foibles of the age; but baseless, unhistorical, irrational, and always endeavouring, in the words of Cardinal Newman,[1] 'to hold the balance between opposites so skilfully as to do without fulcrum or beam.'

In the still more emphatic words of the same high authority, ' the one obvious objection to the whole (High) Anglican line is, *that it is Roman.*'[2]

[1] *Apologia,* p. 193.   [2] *Ibid.* p. 333.

A LIST OF

KEGAN PAUL, TRENCH &

PUBLICATIONS.

1, *Paternoster Square,*
London.

A LIST OF
KEGAN PAUL, TRENCH & CO.'S PUBLICATIONS.

CONTENTS.

	PAGE		PAGE
GENERAL LITERATURE.	2	POETRY.	32
INTERNATIONAL SCIENTIFIC SERIES	27	WORKS OF FICTION	40
		BOOKS FOR THE YOUNG	42
MILITARY WORKS.	30		

GENERAL LITERATURE.

ADAMS, F. O., F.R.G.S.—**The History of Japan.** From the Earliest Period to the Present time. New Edition, revised. 2 vols. With Maps and Plans. Demy 8vo, 21*s.* each.

ADAMSON, H. T., B.D.—**The Truth as it is in Jesus.** Crown 8vo, 8*s.* 6*d.*

The Three Sevens. Crown 8vo, 5*s.* 6*d.*

A. K. H. B.—**From a Quiet Place.** A New Volume of Sermons. Crown 8vo, 5*s.*

ALBERT, Mary.—**Holland and her Heroes to the year 1585.** An Adaptation from "Motley's Rise of the Dutch Republic." Small crown 8vo, 4*s.* 6*d.*

ALLEN, Rev. R., M.A.—**Abraham; his Life, Times, and Travels,** 3,800 years ago. With Map. Second Edition. Post 8vo, 6*s.*

ALLEN, Grant, B.A.—**Physiological Æsthetics.** Large post 8vo, 9*s.*

ALLIES, T. W., M.A.—**Per Crucem ad Lucem.** The Result of a Life. 2 vols. Demy 8vo, 25*s.*

A Life's Decision. Crown 8vo, 7*s.* 6*d.*

ANDERSON, R. C., C.E.—**Tables for Facilitating the Calculation of Every Detail in connection with Earthen and Masonry Dams.** Royal 8vo, £2 2*s.*

ARCHER, Thomas.—About my Father's Business. Work amidst the Sick, the Sad, and the Sorrowing. Cheaper Edition. Crown 8vo, 2*s.* 6*d.*

ARMSTRONG, Richard A., B.A.—Latter-Day Teachers. Six Lectures. Small crown 8vo, 2*s.* 6*d.*

ARNOLD, Arthur.—Social Politics. Demy 8vo, 14*s.*

Free Land. Second Edition. Crown 8vo, 6*s.*

AUBERTIN, J. J.—A Flight to Mexico. With Seven full-page Illustrations and a Railway Map of Mexico. Crown 8vo, 7*s.* 6*d.*

BADGER, George Percy, D.C.L.—An English-Arabic Lexicon. In which the equivalent for English Words and Idiomatic Sentences are rendered into literary and colloquial Arabic. Royal 4to, £9 9*s.*

BAGEHOT, Walter.—The English Constitution. Third Edition. Crown 8vo, 7*s.* 6*d.*

Lombard Street. A Description of the Money Market. Seventh Edition. Crown 8vo, 7*s.* 6*d.*

Some Articles on the Depreciation of Silver, and Topics connected with it. Demy 8vo, 5*s.*

BAGENAL, Philip H.—The American-Irish and their Influence on Irish Politics. Crown 8vo, 5*s.*

BAGOT, Alan, C.E.—Accidents in Mines: Their Causes and Prevention. Crown 8vo, 6*s.*

The Principles of Colliery Ventilation. Second Edition, greatly enlarged. Crown 8vo, 5*s.*

BAKER, Sir Sherston, Bart.—Halleck's International Law; or, Rules Regulating the Intercourse of States in Peace and War. A New Edition, revised, with Notes and Cases. 2 vols. Demy 8vo, 38*s.*

The Laws relating to Quarantine. Crown 8vo, 12*s.* 6*d.*

BALDWIN, Capt. J. H.—The Large and Small Game of Bengal and the North-Western Provinces of India. With numerous Illustrations. Second Edition. 4to, 21*s.*

BALLIN, Ada S. and F. L.—A Hebrew Grammar. With Exercises selected from the Bible. Crown 8vo, 7*s.* 6*d.*

BARCLAY, Edgar.—Mountain Life in Algeria. With numerous Illustrations by Photogravure. Crown 4to, 16*s.*

BARNES, William.—An Outline of English Speechcraft. Crown 8vo, 4*s.*

Outlines of Redecraft (Logic). With English Wording. Crown 8vo, 3*s.*

BARTLEY, G. C. T.—Domestic Economy: Thrift in Every-Day Life. Taught in Dialogues suitable for children of all ages. Small crown 8vo, 2*s.*

BAUR, Ferdinand, Dr. Ph.—A Philological Introduction to Greek and Latin for Students. Translated and adapted from the German, by C. KEGAN PAUL, M.A., and E. D. STONE, M.A. Second Edition. Crown 8vo, 6s.

BAYNES, Rev. Canon R. H.—At the Communion Time. A Manual for Holy Communion. With a preface by the Right Rev. the Lord Bishop of Derry and Raphoe. 1s. 6d.

BELLARS, Rev. W.—The Testimony of Conscience to the Truth and Divine Origin of the Christian Revelation. Burney Prize Essay. Small crown 8vo, 3s. 6d.

BELLINGHAM, Henry, M.P.—Social Aspects of Catholicism and Protestantism in their Civil Bearing upon Nations. Translated and adapted from the French of M. le Baron de Haulleville. With a preface by His Eminence Cardinal Manning. Second and Cheaper Edition. Crown 8vo, 3s. 6d.

BENT, J. Theodore.—Genoa: How the Republic Rose and Fell. With 18 Illustrations. Demy 8vo, 18s.

BLUNT, The Ven. Archdeacon.—The Divine Patriot, and other Sermons. Preached in Scarborough and in Cannes. Crown 8vo, 6s.

BLUNT, Wilfred S.—The Future of Islam. Crown 8vo, 6s.

BONWICK, J., F.R.G.S.—Pyramid Facts and Fancies. Crown 8vo, 5s.

Egyptian Belief and Modern Thought. Large post 8vo, 10s. 6d.

BOUVERIE-PUSEY, S. E. B.—Permanence and Evolution. An Inquiry into the Supposed Mutability of Animal Types. Crown 8vo, 5s.

BOWEN, H. C., M.A.—Studies in English. For the use of Modern Schools. Third Edition. Small crown 8vo, 1s. 6d.

English Grammar for Beginners. Fcap. 8vo, 1s.

BRIDGETT, Rev. T. E.—History of the Holy Eucharist in Great Britain. 2 vols. Demy 8vo, 18s.

BRODRICK, the Hon. G. C.—Political Studies. Demy 8vo, 14s.

BROOKE, Rev. S. A.—Life and Letters of the Late Rev. F. W. Robertson, M.A. Edited by.

    I. Uniform with Robertson's Sermons. 2 vols. With Steel Portrait. 7s. 6d.
    II. Library Edition. With Portrait. 8vo, 12s.
    III. A Popular Edition. In 1 vol., 8vo, 6s.

The Spirit of the Christian Life. A New Volume of Sermons. Second Edition. Crown 8vo, 7s. 6d.

BROOKE, Rev. S. A.—continued.
The Fight of Faith. Sermons preached on various occasions. Fifth Edition. Crown 8vo, 7s. 6d.
Theology in the English Poets.—Cowper, Coleridge, Wordsworth, and Burns. Fourth and Cheaper Edition. Post 8vo, 5s.
Christ in Modern Life. Sixteenth and Cheaper Edition. Crown 8vo, 5s.
Sermons. First Series. Twelfth and Cheaper Edition. Crown 8vo, 5s.
Sermons. Second Series. Fifth and Cheaper Edition. Crown 8vo, 5s.

BROOKE, W. G., M.A.—**The Public Worship Regulation Act.** With a Classified Statement of its Provisions, Notes, and Index. Third Edition, revised and corrected. Crown 8vo, 3s. 6d.
Six Privy Council Judgments.—1850-72. Annotated by. Third Edition. Crown 8vo, 9s.

BROWN, Rev. J. Baldwin, B.A.—**The Higher Life.** Its Reality, Experience, and Destiny. Fifth Edition. Crown 8vo, 5s.
Doctrine of Annihilation in the Light of the Gospel of Love. Five Discourses. Third Edition. Crown 8vo, 2s. 6d.
The Christian Policy of Life. A Book for Young Men of Business. Third Edition. Crown 8vo, 3s. 6d.

BROWN, J. Croumbie, LL.D.—**Reboisement in France;** or, Records of the Replanting of the Alps, the Cevennes, and the Pyrenees with Trees, Herbage, and Bush. Demy 8vo, 12s. 6d.
The Hydrology of Southern Africa. Demy 8vo, 10s. 6d.

BROWN, S. Borton, B.A.—**The Fire Baptism of all Flesh;** or, the Coming Spiritual Crisis of the Dispensation. Crown 8vo, 6s.

BROWNE, W. R.—**The Inspiration of the New Testament.** With a Preface by the Rev. J. P. NORRIS, D.D. Fcap. 8vo, 2s. 6d.

BURCKHARDT, Jacob.—**The Civilization of the Period of the Renaissance in Italy.** Authorized translation, by S. G. C. Middlemore. 2 vols. Demy 8vo, 24s.

BURTON, Mrs. Richard.—**The Inner Life of Syria, Palestine, and the Holy Land.** With Maps, Photographs, and Coloured Plates. Cheaper Edition in one volume. Large post 8vo, 10s. 6d.

BUSBECQ, Ogier Ghiselin de.—**His Life and Letters.** By CHARLES THORNTON FORSTER, M.A., and F. H. BLACKBURNE DANIELL, M.A. 2 vols. With Frontispieces. Demy 8vo, 24s.

CARPENTER, Dr. Phillip P.—**His Life and Work.** Edited by his brother, Russell Lant Carpenter. With Portrait and Vignettes. Second Edition. Crown 8vo, 7s. 6d.

CARPENTER, W. B., LL.D., M.D., F.R.S., etc.—**The Principles of Mental Physiology.** With their Applications to the Training and Discipline of the Mind, and the Study of its Morbid Conditions. Illustrated. Sixth Edition. 8vo, 12s.

CERVANTES.—**The Ingenious Knight Don Quixote de la Mancha.** A New Translation from the Originals of 1605 and 1608. By A. J. DUFFIELD. With Notes. 3 vols. Demy 8vo, 42s.

CHEYNE, Rev. T. K.—**The Prophecies of Isaiah.** Translated with Critical Notes and Dissertations. 2 vols. Second Edition. Demy 8vo, 25s.

CLAIRAUT.—**Elements of Geometry.** Translated by Dr. KAINES. With 145 Figures. Crown 8vo, 4s. 6d.

CLAYDEN, P. W.—**England under Lord Beaconsfield.** The Political History of the Last Six Years, from the end of 1873 to the beginning of 1880. Second Edition, with Index and continuation to March, 1880. Demy 8vo, 16s.

CLODD, Edward, F.R.A.S.—**The Childhood of the World:** a Simple Account of Man in Early Times. Sixth Edition. Crown 8vo, 3s.
    A Special Edition for Schools. 1s.

   The Childhood of Religions. Including a Simple Account of the Birth and Growth of Myths and Legends. Ninth Thousand. Crown 8vo, 5s.
    A Special Edition for Schools. 1s. 6d.

   Jesus of Nazareth. With a brief sketch of Jewish History to the Time of His Birth. Small crown 8vo, 6s.

COGHLAN, J. Cole, D.D.—**The Modern Pharisee and other Sermons.** Edited by the Very Rev. H. H. DICKINSON, D.D., Dean of Chapel Royal, Dublin. New and Cheaper Edition. Crown 8vo, 7s. 6d.

COLERIDGE, Sara.—**Phantasmion.** A Fairy Tale. With an Introductory Preface, by the Right Hon. Lord Coleridge, of Ottery St. Mary. A New Edition. Illustrated. Crown 8vo, 7s. 6d.

   Memoir and Letters of Sara Coleridge. Edited by her Daughter. With Index. Cheap Edition. With one Portrait. 7s. 6d.

Collects Exemplified. Being Illustrations from the Old and New Testaments of the Collects for the Sundays after Trinity. By the Author of "A Commentary on the Epistles and Gospels." Edited by the Rev. JOSEPH JACKSON. Crown 8vo, 5s.

COLLINS, Mortimer.—**The Secret of Long Life.** Small crown 8vo, 3s. 6d.

CONNELL, A. K.—**Discontent and Danger in India.** Small crown 8vo, 3s. 6d.

COOKE, *Prof. J. P.*—Scientific Culture. Crown 8vo, 1*s*.

COOPER, *H. J.*—The Art of Furnishing on Rational and Æsthetic Principles. New and Cheaper Edition. Fcap. 8vo, 1*s*. 6*d*.

CORFIELD, *Prof., M.D.*—Health. Crown 8vo, 6*s*.

CORY, *William.*—A Guide to Modern English History. Part I.—MDCCCXV.-MDCCCXXX. Demy 8vo, 9*s*. Part II.—MDCCCXXX.-MDCCCXXXV., 15*s*.

CORY, *Col. Arthur.*—The Eastern Menace. Crown 8vo, 7*s*. 6*d*.

COTTERILL, *H. B.*—An Introduction to the Study of Poetry. Crown 8vo, 7*s*. 6*d*.

COURTNEY, *W. L.*—The Metaphysics of John Stuart Mill. Crown 8vo, 5*s*. 6*d*.

COX, *Rev. Sir George W., M.A., Bart.*—A History of Greece from the Earliest Period to the end of the Persian War. New Edition. 2 vols. Demy 8vo, 36*s*.

The Mythology of the Aryan Nations. New Edition. Demy 8vo, 16*s*.

A General History of Greece from the Earliest Period to the Death of Alexander the Great, with a sketch of the subsequent History to the present time. New Edition. Crown 8vo, 7*s*. 6*d*.

Tales of Ancient Greece. New Edition. Small crown 8vo, 6*s*.

School History of Greece. New Edition. With Maps. Fcap. 8vo, 3*s*. 6*d*.

The Great Persian War from the History of Herodotus. New Edition. Fcap. 8vo, 3*s*. 6*d*.

A Manual of Mythology in the form of Question and Answer. New Edition. Fcap. 8vo, 3*s*.

An Introduction to the Science of Comparative Mythology and Folk-Lore. Crown 8vo, 9*s*.

COX, *Rev. Sir G. W., M.A., Bart., and JONES, Eustace Hinton.*—Popular Romances of the Middle Ages. Second Edition, in 1 vol. Crown 8vo, 6*s*.

COX, *Rev. Samuel.*—Salvator Mundi ; or, Is Christ the Saviour of all Men? Seventh Edition. Crown 8vo, 5*s*.

The Genesis of Evil, and other Sermons, mainly expository. Second Edition. Crown 8vo, 6*s*.

A Commentary on the Book of Job. With a Translation. Demy 8vo, 15*s*.

CRAUFURD, *A. H.*—Seeking for Light : Sermons. Crown 8vo, 5*s*.

CRAVEN, *Mrs.*—A Year's Meditations. Crown 8vo, 6*s*.

CRAWFURD, *Oswald.*—Portugal, Old and New. With Illustrations and Maps. New and Cheaper Edition. Crown 8vo, 6*s*.

CROZIER, *John Beattie*, *M.B.*—**The Religion of the Future.** Crown 8vo, 6s.

Cyclopædia of Common things. Edited by the Rev. Sir GEORGE W. COX, Bart., M.A. With 500 Illustrations. Third Edition. Large post 8vo, 7s. 6d.

DALTON, *Rev. John Neale*, *M.A.*, *R.N.*—**Sermons to Naval Cadets.** Preached on board H.M.S. "Britannia." Second Edition. Small crown 8vo, 3s. 6d.

DAVIDSON, *Rev. Samuel*, *D.D.*, *LL.D.*—**The New Testament, translated from the Latest Greek Text of Tischendorf.** A New and thoroughly revised Edition. Post 8vo, 10s. 6d.

Canon of the Bible: Its Formation, History, and Fluctuations. Third and revised Edition. Small crown 8vo, 5s.

The Doctrine of Last Things contained in the New Testament compared with the Notions of the Jews and the Statements of Church Creeds. Crown 8vo.

DAVIDSON, *Thomas.*—**The Parthenon Frieze,** and other Essays. Crown 8vo, 6s.

DAVIES, *Rev. J. L.*, *M.A.*—**Theology and Morality.** Essays on Questions of Belief and Practice. Crown 8vo, 7s. 6d.

DAWSON, *Geo.*, *M.A.*—**Prayers, with a Discourse on Prayer.** Edited by his Wife. Eighth Edition. Crown 8vo, 6s.

Sermons on Disputed Points and Special Occasions. Edited by his Wife. Third Edition. Crown 8vo, 6s.

Sermons on Daily Life and Duty. Edited by his Wife. Third Edition. Crown 8vo, 6s.

The Authentic Gospel. A New Volume of Sermons. Edited by GEORGE ST. CLAIR. Second Edition. Crown 8vo, 6s.

DE REDCLIFFE, *Viscount Stratford.*—**Why am I a Christian?** Fifth Edition. Crown 8vo, 3s.

DESPREZ, *Phillip S.*, *B.D.*—**Daniel and John**; or, the Apocalypse of the Old and that of the New Testament. Demy 8vo, 12s.

DIDON, *Rev. Father.*—**Science without God.** Conferences by. Translated from the French by ROSA CORDER. Crown 8vo, cloth, 5s.

DOWDEN, *Edward*, *LL.D.*—**Shakspere:** a Critical Study of his Mind and Art. Sixth Edition. Post 8vo, 12s.

Studies in Literature, 1789–1877. Second and Cheaper Edition. Large post 8vo, 6s.

DREWRY, *G. O.*, *M.D.*—**The Common-Sense Management of the Stomach.** Fifth Edition. Fcap. 8vo, 2s. 6d.

DREWRY, *G. O.*, *M.D.*, *and BARTLETT*, *H. C.*, *Ph.D.*—**Cup and Platter**; or, Notes on Food and its Effects. New and Cheaper Edition. Small 8vo, 1s. 6d.

DUFFIELD, A. J.—Don Quixote: his Critics and Commentators. With a brief account of the minor works of MIGUEL DE CERVANTES SAAVEDRA, and a statement of the aim and end of the greatest of them all. A handy book for general readers. Crown 8vo, 3s. 6d.

DU MONCEL, Count.—The Telephone, the Microphone, and the Phonograph. With 74 Illustrations. Second Edition. Small crown 8vo, 5s.

EDGEWORTH, F. Y.—Mathematical Psychics. An Essay on the Application of Mathematics to Social Science. Demy 8vo, 7s. 6d.

EDIS, Robert W., F.S.A., etc.—Decoration and Furniture of Town Houses: a Series of Cantor Lectures, delivered before the Society of Arts, 1880. Amplified and Enlarged. With 29 Full-page Illustrations and numerous Sketches. Second Edition. Square 8vo, 12s. 6d.

Educational Code of the Prussian Nation, in its Present Form. In accordance with the Decisions of the Common Provincial Law, and with those of Recent Legislation. Crown 8vo, 2s. 6d.

Education Library. Edited by PHILIP MAGNUS :—

    An Introduction to the History of Educational Theories. By OSCAR BROWNING, M.A. Second Edition. 3s. 6d.

    John Amos Comenius: his Life and Educational Work. By Prof. S. S. LAURIE, A.M. 3s. 6d.

    Old Greek Education. By the Rev. Prof. MAHAFFY, M.A. 3s. 6d.

Eighteenth Century Essays. Selected and Edited by AUSTIN DOBSON. With a Miniature Frontispiece by R. Caldecott. Parchment Library Edition, 6s. ; vellum, 7s. 6d.

ELSDALE, Henry.—Studies in Tennyson's Idylls. Crown 8vo, 5s.

ELYOT, Sir Thomas.—The Boke named the Gouernour. Edited from the First Edition of 1531 by HENRY HERBERT STEPHEN CROFT, M.A., Barrister-at-Law. With Portraits of Sir Thomas and Lady Elyot, copied by permission of her Majesty from Holbein's Original Drawings at Windsor Castle. 2 vols. Fcap. 4to, 50s.

Eranus. A Collection of Exercises in the Alcaic and Sapphic Metres. Edited by F. W. CORNISH, Assistant Master at Eton. Crown 8vo, 2s.

EVANS, Mark.—The Story of Our Father's Love, told to Children. Fifth and Cheaper Edition. With Four Illustrations. Fcap. 8vo, 1s. 6d.

EVANS, Mark.—continued.
    A Book of Common Prayer and Worship for Household Use, compiled exclusively from the Holy Scriptures. Second Edition. Fcap. 8vo, 1s.
    The Gospel of Home Life. Crown 8vo, 4s. 6d.
    The King's Story-Book. In Three Parts. Fcap. 8vo, 1s. 6d. each.
    ⁎⁎⁎ Parts I. and II. with Eight Illustrations and Two Picture Maps, now ready.

FELKIN, H. M.—**Technical Education in a Saxon Town.** Published for the City and Guilds of London Institute for the Advancement of Technical Education. Demy 8vo, 2s.

FLOREDICE, W. H.—**A Month among the Mere Irish.** Small crown 8vo, 5s.

Folkestone Ritual Case: the Arguments, Proceedings, Judgment, and Report. Demy 8vo, 25s.

FORMBY, Rev. Henry.—**Ancient Rome and its Connection with the Christian Religion:** An Outline of the History of the City from its First Foundation down to the Erection of the Chair of St. Peter, A.D. 42–47. With numerous Illustrations of Ancient Monuments, Sculpture, and Coinage, and of the Antiquities of the Christian Catacombs. Royal 4to, cloth extra, £2 10s.; roxburgh half-morocco, £2 12s. 6d.

FRASER, Donald.—**Exchange Tables of Sterling and Indian Rupee Currency,** upon a new and extended system, embracing Values from One Farthing to One Hundred Thousand Pounds, and at rates progressing, in Sixteenths of a Penny, from 1s. 9d. to 2s. 3d. per Rupee. Royal 8vo, 10s. 6d.

FRISWELL, J. Hain.—**The Better Self.** Essays for Home Life. Crown 8vo, 6s.

GARDINER, Samuel R., and J. BASS MULLINGER, M.A.—**Introduction to the Study of English History.** Large Crown 8vo, 9s.

GARDNER, Dorsey.—**Quatre Bras, Ligny, and Waterloo.** A Narrative of the Campaign in Belgium, 1815. With Maps and Plans. Demy 8vo, 16s.

GARDNER, J., M.D.—**Longevity: The Means of Prolonging Life after Middle Age.** Fourth Edition, revised and enlarged. Small crown 8vo, 4s.

GEBLER, Karl Von.—**Galileo Galilei and the Roman Curia,** from Authentic Sources. Translated with the sanction of the Author, by Mrs. GEORGE STURGE. Demy 8vo, 12s.

GEDDES, James.—**History of the Administration of John de Witt,** Grand Pensionary of Holland. Vol. I. 1623–1654. With Portrait. Demy 8vo, 15s.

GENNA, E.—Irresponsible Philanthropists. Being some Chapters on the Employment of Gentlewomen. Small crown 8vo, 2s. 6d.

GEORGE, Henry.—Progress and Poverty: an Inquiry into the Causes of Industrial Depressions, and of Increase of Want with Increase of Wealth. The Remedy. Second Edition. Post 8vo, 7s. 6d.

GILBERT, Mrs.—Autobiography and other Memorials. Edited by Josiah Gilbert. Third and Cheaper Edition. With Steel Portrait and several Wood Engravings. Crown 8vo, 7s. 6d.

GLOVER, F., M.A.—Exempla Latina. A First Construing Book, with Short Notes, Lexicon, and an Introduction to the Analysis of Sentences. Fcap. 8vo, 2s.

GODWIN, William.—The Genius of Christianity Unveiled. Being Essays never before published. Edited, with a Preface, by C. Kegan Paul. Crown 8vo, 7s. 6d.

GOLDSMID, Sir Francis Henry, Bart., Q.C., M.P.—Memoir of. With Portrait. Second Edition, revised.. Crown 8vo, 5s.

GOODENOUGH, Commodore J. G.—Memoir of, with Extracts from his Letters and Journals. Edited by his Widow. With Steel Engraved Portrait. Square 8vo, 5s.

*** Also a Library Edition with Maps, Woodcuts, and Steel Engraved Portrait. Square post 8vo, 14s.

GOSSE, Edmund W.—Studies in the Literature of Northern Europe. With a Frontispiece designed and etched by Alma Tadema. Large post 8vo, 12s.

GOULD, Rev. S. Baring, M.A.—The Vicar of Morwenstow: a Memoir of the Rev. R. S. Hawker. With Portrait. Third Edition, revised. Square post 8vo, 10s. 6d.

Germany, Present and Past. New and Cheaper Edition. Large crown 8vo, 7s. 6d.

GOWAN, Major Walter E.—A. Ivanoff's Russian Grammar. (16th Edition.) Translated, enlarged, and arranged for use of Students of the Russian Language. Demy 8vo, 6s.

GRAHAM, William, M.A.—The Creed of Science, Religious, Moral, and Social. Demy 8vo, 12s.

GRIFFITH, Thomas, A.M.—The Gospel of the Divine Life: a Study of the Fourth Evangelist. Demy 8vo, 14s.

GRIMLEY, Rev. H. N., M.A.—Tremadoc Sermons, chiefly on the Spiritual Body, the Unseen World, and the Divine Humanity. Third Edition. Crown 8vo, 6s.

GRÜNER, M.L.—Studies of Blast Furnace Phenomena. Translated by L. D. B. GORDON, F.R.S.E., F.G.S. Demy 8vo, 7s. 6d.

GURNEY, Rev. Archer.—Words of Faith and Cheer. A Mission of Instruction and Suggestion. Crown 8vo, 6s.

HAECKEL, Prof. Ernst.—The History of Creation. Translation revised by Professor E. RAY LANKESTER, M.A., F.R.S. With Coloured Plates and Genealogical Trees of the various groups of both Plants and Animals. 2 vols. Second Edition. Post 8vo, 32s.

The History of the Evolution of Man. With numerous Illustrations. 2 vols. Post 8vo, 32s.

Freedom in Science and Teaching. With a Prefatory Note by T. H. HUXLEY, F.R.S. Crown 8vo, 5s.

HALF-CROWN SERIES :—

Sister Dora : a Biography. By MARGARET LONSDALE.

True Words for Brave Men : a Book for Soldiers and Sailors. By the late CHARLES KINGSLEY.

An Inland Voyage. By R. L. STEVENSON.

Travels with a Donkey. By R. L. STEVENSON.

A Nook in the Apennines. By LEADER SCOTT.

Notes of Travel : being Extracts from the Journals of Count VON MOLTKE.

Letters from Russia. By Count VON MOLTKE.

English Sonnets. Collected and Arranged by J. DENNIS.

Lyrics of Love. From Shakespeare to Tennyson. Selected and Arranged by W. D. ADAMS.

London Lyrics. By F. LOCKER.

Home Songs for Quiet Hours. By the Rev. Canon R. H. BAYNES.

HALLECK'S International Law ; or, Rules Regulating the Intercourse of States in Peace and War. A New Edition, revised with Notes and Cases by Sir SHERSTON BAKER, Bart. 2 vols. Demy 8vo, 38s.

HARTINGTON, The Right Hon. the Marquis of, M.P.—Election Speeches in 1879 and 1880. With Address to the Electors of North-East Lancashire. Crown 8vo, 3s. 6d.

HAWEIS, Rev. H. R., M.A.—Current Coin. Materialism—The Devil—Crime—Drunkenness—Pauperism—Emotion—Recreation—The Sabbath. Fourth and Cheaper Edition. Crown 8vo, 5s.

Arrows in the Air. Fourth and Cheaper Edition. Crown 8vo, 5s.

Speech in Season. Fifth and Cheaper Edition. Crown 8vo, 5s.

Thoughts for the Times. Twelfth and Cheaper Edition. Crown 8vo, 5s.

HAWEIS, Rev. H. R., M.A.—continued.
Unsectarian Family Prayers. New and Cheaper Edition. Fcap. 8vo, 1s. 6d.

HAWKINS, Edwards Comerford.—**Spirit and Form.** Sermons preached in the Parish Church of Leatherhead. Crown 8vo, 6s.

HAYES, A. H., Junr.—**New Colorado, and the Santa Fé Trail.** With Map and 60 Illustrations. Crown 8vo, 9s.

HELLWALD, Baron F. Von.—**The Russians in Central Asia.** A Critical Examination, down to the Present Time, of the Geography and History of Central Asia. Translated by Lieut.-Col. THEODORE WIRGMAN, LL.B. With Map. Large post 8vo, 12s.

HINTON, J.—**The Place of the Physician.** To which is added Essays on the Law of Human Life, and on the Relations between Organic and Inorganic Worlds. Second Edition. Crown 8vo, 3s. 6d.

Philosophy and Religion. Selections from the MSS. of the late JAMES HINTON. Edited by CAROLINE HADDON. Crown 8vo, 5s.

Physiology for Practical Use. By Various Writers. With 50 Illustrations. Third and Cheaper Edition. Crown 8vo, 5s.

An Atlas of Diseases of the Membrana Tympani. With Descriptive Text. Post 8vo, £6 6s.

The Questions of Aural Surgery. With Illustrations. 2 vols. Post 8vo, 12s. 6d.

Chapters on the Art of Thinking, and other Essays. With an Introduction by SHADWORTH HODGSON. Edited by C. H. HINTON. Crown 8vo, 8s. 6d.

The Mystery of Pain. New Edition. Fcap. 8vo, 1s.

Life and Letters. Edited by ELLICE HOPKINS, with an Introduction by Sir W. W. GULL, Bart., and Portrait engraved on Steel by C. H. JEENS. Fourth Edition. Crown 8vo, 8s. 6d.

HOOPER, Mary.—**Little Dinners: How to Serve them with Elegance and Economy.** Thirteenth Edition. Crown 8vo, 5s.

Cookery for Invalids, Persons of Delicate Digestion, and Children. Second Edition. Crown 8vo, 3s. 6d.

Every-Day Meals. Being Economical and Wholesome Recipes for Breakfast, Luncheon, and Supper. Third Edition. Crown 8vo, 5s.

HOPKINS, Ellice.—**Life and Letters of James Hinton,** with an Introduction by Sir W. W. GULL, Bart., and Portrait engraved on Steel by C. H. JEENS. Fourth Edition. Crown 8vo, 8s. 6d.

HORNER, The Misses.—**Walks in Florence.** A New and thoroughly Revised Edition. 2 vols. Crown 8vo. Limp cloth. With Illustrations.
 Vol. I.—Churches, Streets, and Palaces. 10s. 6d.
 Vol. II.—Public Galleries and Museums. 5s.

HOSPITALIER, E.—**The Modern Applications of Electricity.** Translated and Enlarged by Julius Maier, Ph.D. With 170 Illustrations. Demy 8vo, 16s.

Household Readings on Prophecy. By a Layman. Small crown 8vo, 3s. 6d.

HUGHES, Henry.—**The Redemption of the World.** Crown 8vo, 3s. 6d.

HULL, Edmund C. F.—**The European in India.** With a Medical Guide for Anglo-Indians. By R. S. Mair, M.D., F.R.C.S.E. Third Edition, Revised and Corrected. Post 8vo, 6s.

HUNTINGFORD, Rev. E., D.C.L.—**The Apocalypse.** With a Commentary and Introductory Essay. Demy 8vo, 9s.

HUTTON, Arthur, M.A.—**The Anglican Ministry:** Its Nature and Value in relation to the Catholic Priesthood. With a Preface by His Eminence Cardinal Newman. Demy 8vo, 14s.

JENKINS, E., and RAYMOND, J.—**The Architect's Legal Handbook.** Third Edition, Revised. Crown 8vo, 6s.

JENKINS, Rev. R. C., M.A.—**The Privilege of Peter,** and the Claims of the Roman Church confronted with the Scriptures, the Councils, and the Testimony of the Popes themselves. Fcap. 8vo, 3s. 6d.

JENNINGS, Mrs. Vaughan.—**Rahel: Her Life and Letters.** With a Portrait from the Painting by Daffinger. Square post 8vo, 7s. 6d.

JERVIS. Rev. W. Henley.—**The Gallican Church and the Revolution.** A Sequel to the History of the Church of France, from the Concordat of Bologna to the Revolution. Demy 8vo, 18s.

JOEL, L.—**A Consul's Manual and Shipowner's and Shipmaster's Practical Guide in their Transactions Abroad.** With Definitions of Nautical, Mercantile, and Legal Terms; a Glossary of Mercantile Terms in English, French, German, Italian, and Spanish; Tables of the Money, Weights, and Measures of the Principal Commercial Nations and their Equivalents in British Standards; and Forms of Consular and Notarial Acts. Demy 8vo, 12s.

JOHNSTONE, C. F., M.A.—**Historical Abstracts:** being Outlines of the History of some of the less known States of Europe. Crown 8vo, 7s. 6d.

JONCOURT, Madame Marie de.—**Wholesome Cookery.** Crown 8vo, 3s. 6d.

JONES, C. A.—**The Foreign Freaks of Five Friends.** With 30 Illustrations. Crown 8vo, 6s.

JONES, Lucy.—**Puddings and Sweets**; being Three Hundred and Sixty-five Receipts approved by experience. Crown 8vo, 2s. 6d.

JOYCE, P. W., LL.D., etc.—**Old Celtic Romances.** Translated from the Gaelic. Crown 8vo, 7s. 6d.

KAUFMANN, Rev. M., B.A.—**Socialism**: Its Nature, its Dangers, and its Remedies considered. Crown 8vo, 7s. 6d.

Utopias; or, Schemes of Social Improvement, from Sir Thomas More to Karl Marx. Crown 8vo, 5s.

KAY, Joseph.—**Free Trade in Land.** Edited by his Widow. With Preface by the Right Hon. JOHN BRIGHT, M.P. Sixth Edition. Crown 8vo, 5s.

KEMPIS, Thomas à.—**Of the Imitation of Christ.** Parchment Library Edition, 6s.; or vellum, 7s. 6d. The Red Line Edition, fcap. 8vo, red edges, 2s. 6d. The Cabinet Edition, small 8vo, cloth limp, 1s.; cloth boards, red edges, 1s. 6d. The Miniature Edition, red edges, 32mo, 1s.

*** All the above Editions may be had in various extra bindings.

KENT, C.—**Corona Catholica ad Petri successoris Pedes Oblata. De Summi Pontificis Leonis XIII. Assumptione Epigramma.** In Quinquaginta Linguis. Fcap. 4to, 15s.

KERNER, Dr. A.—**Flowers and their Unbidden Guests.** Translation edited by W. OGLE, M.A., M.D. With Illustrations. Square 8vo, 9s.

KETTLEWELL, Rev. S.—**Thomas à Kempis and the Brothers of Common Life.** 2 vols. With Frontispieces. Demy 8vo, 30s.

KIDD, Joseph, M.D.—**The Laws of Therapeutics**; or, the Science and Art of Medicine. Second Edition. Crown 8vo, 6s.

KINAHAN, G. Henry, M.R.I.A.—**The Geology of Ireland**, with numerous Illustrations and a Geological Map of Ireland. Square 8vo, 15s.

KINGSFORD, Anna, M.D.—**The Perfect Way in Diet.** A Treatise advocating a Return to the Natural and Ancient Food of our Race. Small crown 8vo, 2s.

KINGSLEY, Charles, M.A.—**Letters and Memories of his Life.** Edited by his Wife. With two Steel Engraved Portraits, and Vignettes on Wood. Eleventh Cabinet Edition. 2 vols. Crown 8vo, 12s.

All Saints' Day, and other Sermons. Edited by the Rev. W. HARRISON. Third Edition. Crown 8vo, 7s. 6d.

True Words for Brave Men. A Book for Soldiers' and Sailors' Libraries. Eighth Edition. Crown 8vo, 2s. 6d.

KNIGHT, Professor W.—Studies in Philosophy and Literature. Large Post 8vo, 7s. 6d.

KNOX, Alexander A.—The New Playground; or, Wanderings in Algeria. Large crown 8vo, 10s. 6d.

LAURIE, S. S.—The Training of Teachers, and other Educational Papers. Crown 8vo, 7s. 6d.

LEE, Rev. F. G., D.C.L.—The Other World; or, Glimpses of the Supernatural. 2 vols. A New Edition. Crown 8vo, 15s.

LEWIS, Edward Dillon.—A Draft Code of Criminal Law and Procedure. Demy 8vo, 21s.

LINDSAY, W. Lauder, M.D.—Mind in the Lower Animals in Health and Disease. 2 vols. Demy 8vo, 32s.
Vol. I.—Mind in Health. Vol. II.—Mind in Disease.

LLOYD, Walter.—The Hope of the World: An Essay on Universal Redemption. Crown 8vo, 5s.

LONSDALE, Margaret.—Sister Dora: a Biography. With Portrait. Twenty-fifth Edition. Crown 8vo, 2s. 6d.

LORIMER, Peter, D.D.—John Knox and the Church of England. His Work in her Pulpit, and his Influence upon her Liturgy, Articles, and Parties. Demy 8vo, 12s.

John Wiclif and his English Precursors. By GERHARD VICTOR LECHLER. Translated from the German, with additional Notes. New and Cheaper Edition. Demy 8vo, 10s. 6d.

LOWDER, Charles.—A Biography. By the Author of "St. Teresa." Sixth Edition. Large crown 8vo. With Portrait. 7s. 6d.

MACHIAVELLI, Niccoli. The Prince. Translated from the Italian by N. H. T. Small crown 8vo, printed on hand-made paper, bevelled boards, 6s.

MACKENZIE, Alexander.—How India is Governed. Being an Account of England's work in India. Small crown 8vo, 2s.

MACNAUGHT, Rev. John.—Cœna Domini: An Essay on the Lord's Supper, its Primitive Institution, Apostolic Uses, and Subsequent History. Demy 8vo, 14s.

MAGNUS, Mrs.—About the Jews since Bible Times. From the Babylonian Exile till the English Exodus. Small crown 8vo, 5s.

MAIR, R. S., M.D., F.R.C.S.E.—The Medical Guide for Anglo-Indians. Being a Compendium of Advice to Europeans in India, relating to the Preservation and Regulation of Health. With a Supplement on the Management of Children in India. Second Edition. Crown 8vo, limp cloth, 3s. 6d.

MANNING, His Eminence Cardinal.—The True Story of the Vatican Council. Crown 8vo, 5s.

MARKHAM, Capt. Albert Hastings, R.N.—The Great Frozen Sea :
A Personal Narrative of the Voyage of the *Alert* during the Arctic
Expedition of 1875-6. With 6 Full-page Illustrations, 2 Maps,
and 27 Woodcuts. Fifth and Cheaper Edition. Crown 8vo, 6s.

A Polar Reconnaissance : being the Voyage of the *Isbjörn*
to Novaya Zemlya in 1879. With 10 Illustrations. Demy 8vo, 16s.

Marriage and Maternity ; or, Scripture Wives and Mothers. Small
crown 8vo, 4s. 6d.

MARTINEAU, Gertrude.—Outline Lessons on Morals. Small
crown 8vo, 3s. 6d.

McGRATH, Terence.—Pictures from Ireland. New and Cheaper
Edition. Crown 8vo, 2s.

MEREDITH, M.A.—Theotokos, the Example for Woman.
Dedicated, by permission, to Lady AGNES WOOD. Revised by
the Venerable Archdeacon DENISON. 32mo, limp cloth, 1s. 6d.

MERRITT, Henry.—Art-Criticism and Romance. With Recollections and 23 Illustrations in *eau-forte*, by Anna Lea
Merritt. 2 vols. Large post 8vo, 25s.

MILLER, Edward.—The History and Doctrines of Irvingism ;
or, the so-called Catholic and Apostolic Church. 2 vols. Large
post 8vo, 25s.

The Church in Relation to the State. Large crown 8vo,
7s. 6d.

MILNE, James.—Tables of Exchange for the Conversion of Sterling
Money into Indian and Ceylon Currency, at Rates from 1s. 8d. to
2s. 3d. per Rupee. Second Edition. Demy 8vo, £2 2s.

MINCHIN, J. G.—Bulgaria since the War : Notes of a Tour in
the Autumn of 1879. Small crown 8vo, 3s. 6d.

MOCKLER, E.—A Grammar of the Baloochee Language, as
it is spoken in Makran (Ancient Gedrosia), in the Persia-Arabic
and Roman characters. Fcap. 8vo, 5s.

MOLESWORTH, Rev. W. Nassau, M.A.—History of the Church
of England from 1660. Large crown 8vo, 7s. 6d.

MORELL, J. R.—Euclid Simplified in Method and Language.
Being a Manual of Geometry. Compiled from the most important
French Works, approved by the University of Paris and the
Minister of Public Instruction. Fcap. 8vo, 2s. 6d.

MORSE, E. S., Ph.D.—First Book of Zoology. With numerous
Illustrations. New and Cheaper Edition. Crown 8vo, 2s. 6d.

MUNRO, Major-Gen. Sir Thomas, Bart., K.C.B., Governor of Madras.
—SELECTIONS FROM HIS MINUTES AND OTHER OFFICIAL
WRITINGS. Edited, with an Introductory Memoir, by Sir ALEXANDER ARBUTHNOT, K.C.S.I., C.I.E. 2 vols. Demy 8vo, 30s.

NELSON, J. H., M.A.—A Prospectus of the Scientific Study
of the Hindû Law. Demy 8vo, 9s.

NEWMAN, J. H., D.D.—**Characteristics from the Writings of.** Being Selections from his various Works. Arranged with the Author's personal Approval. Sixth Edition. With Portrait. Crown 8vo, 6*s*.

** A Portrait of the Rev. Dr. J. H. Newman, mounted for framing, can be had, 2*s*. 6*d*.

New Werther. By LOKI. Small crown 8vo, 2*s*. 6*d*.

NICHOLSON, Edward Byron.—**The Gospel according to the Hebrews.** Its Fragments Translated and Annotated with a Critical Analysis of the External and Internal Evidence relating to it. Demy 8vo, 9*s*. 6*d*.

A New Commentary on the Gospel according to Matthew. Demy 8vo, 12*s*.

The Rights of an Animal. Crown 8vo, 3*s*. 6*d*.

NICOLS, Arthur, F.G.S., F.R.G.S.—**Chapters from the Physical History of the Earth:** an Introduction to Geology and Palæontology. With numerous Illustrations. Crown 8vo, 5*s*.

Notes on St. Paul's Epistle to the Galatians. For Readers of the Authorised Version or the Original Greek. Demy 8vo, 2*s*. 6*d*.

Nuces: EXERCISES ON THE SYNTAX OF THE PUBLIC SCHOOL LATIN PRIMER. New Edition in Three Parts. Crown 8vo, each 1*s*.

** The Three Parts can also be had bound together, 3*s*.

OATES, Frank, F.R.G.S.—**Matabele Land and the Victoria Falls.** A Naturalist's Wanderings in the Interior of South Africa. Edited by C. G. OATES, B.A. With numerous Illustrations and 4 Maps. Demy 8vo, 21*s*.

OGLE, W., M.D., F.R.C.P.—**Aristotle on the Parts of Animals.** Translated, with Introduction and Notes. Royal 8vo, 12*s*. 6*d*.

O'MEARA, Kathleen.—**Frederic Ozanam,** Professor of the Sorbonne: His Life and Work. Second Edition. Crown 8vo, 7*s*. 6*d*.

Henri Perreyve and his Counsels to the Sick. Small crown 8vo, 5*s*.

Our Public Schools—Eton, Harrow, Winchester, Rugby, Westminster, Marlborough, The Charterhouse. Crown 8vo, 6*s*.

OWEN, F. M.—**John Keats:** a Study. Crown 8vo, 6*s*.

OWEN, Rev. Robert, B.D.—**Sanctorale Catholicum; or, Book of Saints.** With Notes, Critical, Exegetical, and Historical. Demy 8vo, 18*s*.

An Essay on the Communion of Saints. Including an Examination of the Cultus Sanctorum. 2*s*.

OXENHAM, Rev. F. Nutcombe.—**What is the Truth as to Everlasting Punishment.** Part II. Being an Historical Inquiry into the Witness and Weight of certain Anti-Origenist Councils. Crown 8vo, 2*s*. 6*d*.

** Parts I. and II. complete in one volume, 7*s*.

Parchment Library. Choicely Printed on hand-made paper, limp parchment antique, 6s. ; vellum, 7s. 6d. each volume.

The Christian Year. Thoughts in Verse for the Sundays and Holy Days throughout the Year. With Miniature Portrait of the Rev. J. Keble, after a Drawing by G. Richmond, R.A.

Shakspere's Works. Now publishing in Twelve Monthly Volumes.

Eighteenth Century Essays. Selected and Edited by AUSTIN DOBSON. With a Miniature Frontispiece by R. Caldecott.

Q. Horati Flacci Opera. Edited by F. A. CORNISH, Assistant Master at Eton. With a Frontispiece after a design by L. ALMA TADEMA, etched by Leopold Lowenstam.

Edgar Allan Poe's Poems. With an Essay on his Poetry by ANDREW LANG, and a Frontispiece by Linley Sambourne.

Shakspere's Sonnets. Edited by EDWARD DOWDEN. With a Frontispiece etched by Leopold Lowenstam, after the Death Mask.

English Odes. Selected by EDMUND W. GOSSE. With Frontispiece on India paper by Hamo Thornycroft, A.R.A.

Of the Imitation of Christ. By THOMAS À KEMPIS. A revised Translation. With Frontispiece on India paper, from a Design by W. B. Richmond.

Tennyson's The Princess: a Medley. With a Miniature Frontispiece by H. M. Paget, and a Tailpiece in Outline by Gordon Browne.

Poems: Selected from PERCY BYSSHE SHELLEY. Dedicated to Lady Shelley. With a Preface by RICHARD GARNET and a Miniature Frontispiece.

Tennyson's "In Memoriam." With a Miniature Portrait in *eau-forte* by Le Rat, after a Photograph by the late Mrs. Cameron.

Gay's Fables. With an Introduction by AUSTIN DOBSON.
In the Press.

French Lyrics. Selected and Annotated by G. SAINTSBURY.
In the Press.

Select Letters of Percy Bysshe Shelley. Edited, with an Introduction, by RICHARD GARNETT. *In the Press.*

PARKER, Joseph, D.D.—**The Paraclete:** An Essay on the Personality and Ministry of the Holy Ghost, with some reference to current discussions. Second Edition. Demy 8vo, 12s.

PARR, Capt. H. Hallam, C.M.G.—**A Sketch of the Kafir and Zulu Wars:** Guadana to Isandhlwana. With Maps. Small crown 8vo, 5s.

PARSLOE, Joseph.—**Our Railways.** Sketches, Historical and Descriptive. With Practical Information as to Fares and Rates, etc., and a Chapter on Railway Reform. Crown 8vo, 6s.

PATTISON, Mrs. Mark.—The Renaissance of Art in France. With Nineteen Steel Engravings. 2 vols. Demy 8vo, 32s.

PEARSON, Rev. S.—Week-day Living. A Book for Young Men and Women. Second Edition. Crown 8vo, 5s.

PENRICE, Maj. J., B.A.—A Dictionary and Glossary of the Ko-ran. With Copious Grammatical References and Explanations of the Text. 4to, 21s.

PESCHEL, Dr. Oscar.—The Races of Man and their Geographical Distribution. Large crown 8vo, 9s.

PETERS, F. A.—The Nicomachean Ethics of Aristotle. Translated by. Crown 8vo, 6s.

PIDGEON, D.—An Engineer's Holiday; or, Notes of a Round Trip from Long. 0° to 0°. 2 vols. Large crown 8vo, 16s.

PLAYFAIR, Lieut.-Col.—Travels in the Footsteps of Bruce in Algeria and Tunis. Illustrated by facsimiles of Bruce's original Drawings, Photographs, Maps, etc. Royal 4to cloth, bevelled boards, gilt leaves, £3 3s.

POLLOCK, Frederick.—Spinoza, his Life and Philosophy. Demy 8vo, 16s.

POLLOCK, W. H.—Lectures on French Poets. Delivered at the Royal Institution. Small crown 8vo, 5s.

POOR, Laura E.—Sanskrit and its Kindred Literatures. Studies in Comparative Mythology. Small crown 8vo, 5s.

PRICE, Prof. Bonamy.—Currency and Banking. Crown 8vo, 6s.

Chapters on Practical Political Economy. Being the Substance of Lectures delivered before the University of Oxford. New and Cheaper Edition. Large post 8vo, 5s.

Proteus and Amadeus. A Correspondence. Edited by AUBREY DE VERE. Crown 8vo, 5s.

Pulpit Commentary, The. Edited by the Rev. J. S. EXELL and the Rev. Canon H. D. M. SPENCE.

Genesis. By the Rev. T. WHITELAW, M.A.; with Homilies by the Very Rev. J. F. MONTGOMERY, D.D., Rev. Prof. R. A. REDFORD, M.A., LL.B., Rev. F. HASTINGS, Rev. W. ROBERTS, M.A. An Introduction to the Study of the Old Testament by the Rev. Canon FARRAR, D.D., F.R.S.; and Introductions to the Pentateuch by the Right Rev. H. COTTERILL, D.D., and Rev. T. WHITELAW, M.A. Sixth Edition. 1 vol., 15s.

Exodus. By the Rev. Canon RAWLINSON. With Homilies by Rev. J. ORR, Rev. D. YOUNG, Rev. C. A. GOODHART, Rev. J. URQUHART, and the Rev. H. T. ROBJOHNS. Second Edition. 16s.

Pulpit Commentary, The.—*continued.*
  Leviticus. By the Rev. Prebendary MEYRICK, M.A. With Introductions by the Rev. R. COLLINS, Rev. Professor A. CAVE, and Homilies by Rev. Prof. REDFORD, LL.B., Rev. J. A. MACDONALD, Rev. W. CLARKSON, Rev. S. R. ALDRIDGE, LL.B., and Rev. MCCHEYNE EDGAR. Third Edition. 15s.
  Numbers. By the Rev. R. WINTERBOTHAM, LL.B.; with Homilies by the Rev. Professor W. BINNIE, D.D., Rev. E. S. PROUT, M.A., Rev. D. YOUNG, Rev. J. WAITE, and an Introduction by the Rev. THOMAS WHITELAW, M.A. Third Edition. 15s.
  Deuteronomy. By the Rev. W. L. ALEXANDER, D.D. With Homilies by Rev. C. Clemance, D.D., Rev. J. Orr, B.D., Rev. R. M. Edgar, M.A., Rev. D. Davies, M.A. Price 15s.
  Joshua. By Rev. J. J. LIAS, M.A.; with Homilies by Rev. S. R. ALDRIDGE, LL.B., Rev. R. GLOVER, REV. E. DE PRESSENSÉ, D.D., Rev. J. WAITE, B.A., Rev. F. W. ADENEY, M.A.; and an Introduction by the Rev. A. PLUMMER, M.A. Fourth Edition. 12s. 6d.
  Judges and Ruth. By the Right Rev. Lord A. C. HERVEY, D.D., and Rev. J. MORRISON, D.D.; with Homilies by Rev. A. F. MUIR, M.A., Rev. W. F. ADENEY, M.A., Rev. W. M. STATHAM, and Rev. Professor J. THOMSON, M.A. Third Edition. 10s. 6d.
  1 Samuel. By the Very Rev. R. P. SMITH, D.D.; with Homilies by Rev. DONALD FRASER, D.D., Rev. Prof. CHAPMAN, and Rev. B. DALE. Fourth Edition. 15s.
  1 Kings. By the Rev. JOSEPH HAMMOND, LL.B. With Homilies by the Rev. E. DE PRESSENSÉ, D.D., Rev. J. WAITE, B.A., Rev. A. ROWLAND, LL.B., Rev. J. A. MACDONALD, and Rev. J. URQUHART. Third Edition. 15s.
  Ezra, Nehemiah, and Esther. By Rev. Canon G. RAWLINSON, M.A.; with Homilies by Rev. Prof. J. R. THOMSON, M.A., Rev. Prof. R. A. REDFORD, LL.B., M.A., Rev. W. S. LEWIS, M.A., Rev. J. A. MACDONALD, Rev. A. MACKENNAL, B.A., Rev. W. CLARKSON, B.A., Rev. F. HASTINGS, Rev. W. DINWIDDIE, LL.B., Rev. Prof. ROWLANDS, B.A., Rev. G. WOOD, B.A., Rev. Prof. P. C. BARKER, LL.B., M.A., and the Rev. J. S. EXELL. Fifth Edition. 1 vol., 12s. 6d.
  Punjaub, The, and North-Western Frontier of India. By an Old Punjaubee. Crown 8vo, 5s.
  Rabbi Jeshua. An Eastern Story. Crown 8vo, 3s. 6d.
  RADCLIFFE, Frank R. Y.—**The New Politicus.** Small crown 8vo, 2s. 6d.
  RAVENSHAW, John Henry, B.C.S.—**Gaur: Its Ruins and Inscriptions.** Edited by his Widow. With 44 Photographic Illustrations, and 25 facsimiles of Inscriptions. Royal 4to, £3 13s. 6d.

READ, Carveth.—On the Theory of Logic: An Essay. Crown 8vo, 6s.

Realities of the Future Life. Small crown 8vo, 1s. 6d.

RENDELL, J. M.—Concise Handbook of the Island of Madeira. With Plan of Funchal and Map of the Island. Fcap. 8vo, 1s. 6d.

REYNOLDS, Rev. J. W.—The Supernatural in Nature. A Verification by Free Use of Science. Second Edition, revised and enlarged. Demy 8vo, 14s.

The Mystery of Miracles. New and Enlarged Edition. Crown 8vo, 6s.

RIBOT, Prof. Th.—English Psychology. Second Edition. A Revised and Corrected Translation from the latest French Edition. Large post 8vo, 9s.

Heredity: A Psychological Study on its Phenomena, its Laws, its Causes, and its Consequences. Large crown 8vo, 9s.

ROBERTSON, The late Rev. F. W., M.A.—Life and Letters of. Edited by the Rev. Stopford Brooke, M.A.
    I. Two vols., uniform with the Sermons. With Steel Portrait. Crown 8vo, 7s. 6d.
    II. Library Edition, in Demy 8vo, with Portrait. 12s.
    III. A Popular Edition, in 1 vol. Crown 8vo, 6s.

Sermons. Four Series. Small crown 8vo, 3s. 6d. each.

The Human Race, and other Sermons. Preached at Cheltenham, Oxford, and Brighton. Large post 8vo, 7s. 6d.

Notes on Genesis. New and Cheaper Edition. Crown 8vo, 3s. 6d.

Expository Lectures on St. Paul's Epistles to the Corinthians. A New Edition. Small crown 8vo, 5s.

Lectures and Addresses, with other Literary Remains. A New Edition. Crown 8vo, 5s.

An Analysis of Mr. Tennyson's "In Memoriam." (Dedicated by Permission to the Poet-Laureate.) Fcap. 8vo, 2s.

The Education of the Human Race. Translated from the German of Gotthold Ephraim Lessing. Fcap. 8vo, 2s. 6d.

The above Works can also be had, bound in half morocco.

** A Portrait of the late Rev. F. W. Robertson, mounted for framing, can be had, 2s. 6d.

RODWELL, G. F., F.R.A.S., F.C.S.—Etna: A History of the Mountain and its Eruptions. With Maps and Illustrations. Square 8vo, 9s.

ROLLESTON, T. W. H., B.A.—The Encheiridion of Epictetus. Translated from the Greek, with a Preface and Notes. Small crown 8vo, 3s. 6d.

Rosmini's Philosophical System. Translated, with a Sketch of the Author's Life, Bibliography, Introduction, and Notes by THOMAS DAVIDSON. Demy 8vo, 16s.

SALTS, Rev. Alfred, LL.D.—**Godparents at Confirmation.** With a Preface by the Bishop of Manchester. Small crown 8vo, limp cloth, 2s.

SALVATOR, Archduke Ludwig.—**Levkosia, the Capital of Cyprus.** Crown 4to, 10s. 6d.

SAMUEL, Sydney M.—**Jewish Life in the East.** Small crown 8vo, 3s. 6d.

SAYCE, Rev. Archibald Henry.—**Introduction to the Science of Language.** 2 vols. Large post 8vo, 25s.

Scientific Layman. The New Truth and the Old Faith: are they Incompatible? Demy 8vo, 10s. 6d.

SCOONES, W. Baptiste.—**Four Centuries of English Letters:** A Selection of 350 Letters by 150 Writers, from the Period of the Paston Letters to the Present Time. Second Edition. Large crown 8vo, 9s.

SCOTT, Robert H.—**Weather Charts and Storm Warnings.** Second Edition. Illustrated. Crown 8vo, 3s. 6d.

SHAKSPEARE, Charles.—**Saint Paul at Athens.** Spiritual Christianity in relation to some aspects of Modern Thought. Five Sermons preached at St. Stephen's Church, Westbourne Park. With a Preface by the Rev. Canon FARRAR. Crown 8vo, 5s.

SHELLEY, Lady.—**Shelley Memorials from Authentic Sources.** With (now first printed) an Essay on Christianity by Percy Bysshe Shelley. With Portrait. Third Edition. Crown 8vo, 5s.

SHILLITO, Rev. Joseph.—**Womanhood:** its Duties, Temptations, and Privileges. A Book for Young Women. Third Edition. Crown 8vo, 3s. 6d.

SHIPLEY, Rev. Orby, M.A.—**Church Tracts: or, Studies in Modern Problems.** By various Writers. 2 vols. Crown 8vo, 5s. each.

Principles of the Faith in Relation to Sin. Topics for Thought in Times of Retreat. Eleven Addresses delivered during a Retreat of Three Days to Persons living in the World. Demy 8vo, 12s.

Sister Augustine, Superior of the Sisters of Charity at the St. Johannis Hospital at Bonn. Authorised Translation by HANS THARAU, from the German "Memorials of AMALIE VON LASAULX." Second Edition. Large crown 8vo, 7s. 6d.

SMITH, Edward, M.D., LL.B., F.R.S.—**Health and Disease,** as Influenced by the Daily, Seasonal, and other Cyclical Changes in the Human System. A New Edition. Post 8vo, 7s. 6d.

SMITH, *Edward, M.D., LL.B., F.R.S.—continued.*
>Practical Dietary for Families, Schools, and the Labouring Classes. A New Edition. Post 8vo, 3s. 6d.
>
>Tubercular Consumption in its Early and Remediable Stages. Second Edition. Crown 8vo, 6s.

SPEDDING, *James.*—Reviews and Discussions, Literary, Political, and Historical not relating to Bacon. Demy 8vo, 12s. 6d.
>Evenings with a Reviewer; or, Bacon and Macaulay. With a Prefatory Notice by G. S. VENABLES, Q.C. 2 vols. Demy 8vo, 18s.

STAPFER, *Paul.*—Shakspeare and Classical Antiquity: Greek and Latin Antiquity as presented in Shakspeare's Plays. Translated by EMILY J. CAREY. Large post 8vo, 12s.

ST. BERNARD.—A Little Book on the Love of God. Translated by MARIANNE CAROLINE and COVENTRY PATMORE. Extra, gilt top, 4s. 6d.

STEPHENS, *Archibald John, LL.D.*—The Folkestone Ritual Case. The Substance of the Argument delivered before the Judicial Committee of the Privy Council on behalf of the Respondents. Demy 8vo, 6s.

STEVENSON, *Rev. W. F.*—Hymns for the Church and Home. Selected and Edited by the Rev. W. Fleming Stevenson.
>The Hymn Book consists of Three Parts:—I. For Public Worship.—II. For Family and Private Worship.—III. For Children.
>
>*** Published in various forms and prices, the latter ranging from 8d. to 6s.
>
>Lists and full particulars will be furnished on application to the Publishers.

STEVENSON, *Robert Louis.*—Travels with a Donkey in the Cevennes. With Frontispiece by Walter Crane. Small crown 8vo, 2s. 6d.
>An Inland Voyage. With Frontispiece by Walter Crane. Small Crown 8vo, 2s. 6d.
>
>Virginibus Puerisque, and other Papers. Crown 8vo, 6s.

STRACHEY, *Sir John, G.C.S.I.,* and *Lieut.-Gen. Richard* STRACHEY, *R.E., F.R.S.*—The Finances and Public Works of India, from 1869 to 1881. Demy 8vo, 18s.

STRECKER-WISLICENUS.—Organic Chemistry. Translated and Edited, with Extensive Additions, by W. R. HODGKINSON, Ph.D., and A. J. GREENAWAY, F.I.C. Demy 8vo, 21s.

SULLY, *James, M.A.*—Sensation and Intuition. Demy 8vo, 10s. 6d.

SULLY, James, M.A.—continued.
Pessimism : a History and a Criticism. Second Edition. Demy 8vo, 14s.

SYME, David.—Outlines of an Industrial Science. Second Edition. Crown 8vo, 6s.
Representative Government in England. Its Faults and Failures. Second Edition. Large crown 8vo, 6s.

TAYLOR, Algernon.—Guienne. Notes of an Autumn Tour. Crown 8vo, 4s. 6d.

THOMSON, J. Turnbull.—Social Problems; or, An Inquiry into the Laws of Influence. With Diagrams. Demy 8vo, 10s. 6d.

TIDMAN, Paul F.—Gold and Silver Money. Part I.—A Plain Statement. Part II.—Objections Answered. Third Edition. Crown 8vo, 1s.

TODHUNTER, Dr. J.—A Study of Shelley. Crown 8vo, 7s.

TREMENHEERE, Hugh Seymour, C.B.— A Manual of the Principles of Government, as set forth by the Authorities of Ancient and Modern Times. New and enlarged Edition. Crown 8vo, 5s.

TUKE, Daniel Hack, M.D., F.R.C.P.—Chapters in the History of the Insane in the British Isles. With 4 Illustrations. Demy 8vo, 12s.

TWINING, Louisa.—Workhouse Visiting and Management during Twenty-Five Years. Small crown 8vo, 3s. 6d.

UPTON, Major R. D.—Gleanings from the Desert of Arabia. Large post 8vo, 10s. 6d.

VACUUS, Viator.—Flying South. Recollections of France and its Littoral. Small crown 8vo, 3s. 6d.

VAUGHAN, H. Halford.—New Readings and Renderings of Shakespeare's Tragedies. 2 vols. Demy 8vo, 25s.

VILLARI, Professor.—Niccolo Machiavelli and his Times. Translated by Linda Villari. 2 vols. Large post 8vo, 24s.

VOLCKXSOM, E. W. V.—Catechism of Elementary Modern Chemistry. Small crown 8vo, 3s.

VYNER, Lady Mary.—Every Day a Portion. Adapted from the Bible and the Prayer Book, for the Private Devotion of those living in Widowhood. Collected and Edited by Lady Mary Vyner. Square crown 8vo, 5s.

WALDSTEIN, Charles, Ph.D.—The Balance of Emotion and Intellect; an Introductory Essay to the Study of Philosophy. Crown 8vo, 6s.

WALLER, Rev. C. B.—The Apocalypse, reviewed under the Light of the Doctrine of the Unfolding Ages, and the Restitution of All Things. Demy 8vo, 12*s.*

WALPOLE, Chas. George.—History of Ireland from the Earliest Times to the Union with Great Britain. With 5 Maps and Appendices. Crown 8vo, 10*s.* 6*d.*

WALSHE, Walter Hayle, M.D.—Dramatic Singing Physiologically Estimated. Crown 8vo, 3*s.* 6*d.*

WATSON, Sir Thomas, Bart., M.D.—The Abolition of Zymotic Diseases, and of other similar Enemies of Mankind. Small crown 8vo, 3*s.* 6*d.*

WEDMORE, Frederick.—The Masters of Genre Painting. With Sixteen Illustrations. Crown 8vo, 7*s.* 6*d.*

WHEWELL, William, D.D.—His Life and Selections from his Correspondence. By Mrs. STAIR DOUGLAS. With a Portrait from a Painting by SAMUEL LAURENCE. Demy 8vo, 21*s.*

WHITE, A. D., LL.D.—Warfare of Science. With Prefatory Note by Professor Tyndall. Second Edition. Crown 8vo, 3*s.* 6*d.*

WHITNEY, Prof. William Dwight.—Essentials of English Grammar, for the Use of Schools. Crown 8vo, 3*s.* 6*d.*

WICKSTEED, P. H.—Dante: Six Sermons. Crown 8vo, 5*s.*

WILLIAMS, Rowland, D.D.—Psalms, Litanies, Counsels, and Collects for Devout Persons. Edited by his Widow. New and Popular Edition. Crown 8vo, 3*s.* 6*d.*

Stray Thoughts Collected from the Writings of the late Rowland Williams, D.D. Edited by his Widow. Crown 8vo, 3*s.* 6*d.*

WILLIS, R., M.D.—Servetus and Calvin: a Study of an Important Epoch in the Early History of the Reformation. 8vo, 16*s.*

William Harvey. A History of the Discovery of the Circulation of the Blood: with a Portrait of Harvey after Faithorne. Demy 8vo, 14*s.*

WILSON, Sir Erasmus.—Egypt of the Past. With Chromo-lithograph and numerous Illustrations in the text. Second Edition, Revised. Crown 8vo, 12*s.*

WILSON, H. Schütz.—The Tower and Scaffold. A Miniature Monograph. Large fcap. 8vo, 1*s.*

WOLLSTONECRAFT, Mary.—Letters to Imlay. New Edition, with a Prefatory Memoir by C. KEGAN PAUL. Two Portraits in *eau-forte* by Anna Lea Merritt. Crown 8vo, 6*s.*

WOLTMANN, *Dr. Alfred, and* **WOERMANN**, *Dr. Karl.*—History of Painting. Edited by Sidney Colvin. Vol. I. Painting in Antiquity and the Middle Ages. With numerous Illustrations. Medium 8vo, 28s. ; bevelled boards, gilt leaves, 30s.

WOOD, *Major-General J. Creighton.*—Doubling the Consonant. Small crown 8vo, 1s. 6d.

Word was Made Flesh. Short Family Readings on the Epistles for each Sunday of the Christian Year. Demy 8vo, 10s. 6d.

WREN, *Sir Christopher.*—His Family and His Times. With Original Letters, and a Discourse on Architecture hitherto unpublished. By LUCY PHILLIMORE. With Portrait. Demy 8vo, 14s.

WRIGHT, *Rev. David, M.A.*—Waiting for the Light, and other Sermons. Crown 8vo, 6s.

YOUMANS, *Eliza A.*—An Essay on the Culture of the Observing Powers of Children, especially in connection with the Study of Botany. Edited, with Notes and a Supplement, by Joseph Payne, F.C.P., Author of "Lectures on the Science and Art of Education," etc. Crown 8vo, 2s. 6d.

First Book of Botany. Designed to Cultivate the Observing Powers of Children. With 300 Engravings. New and Cheaper Edition. Crown 8vo, 2s. 6d.

YOUMANS, *Edward L., M.D.*—A Class Book of Chemistry, on the Basis of the New System. With 200 Illustrations. Crown 8vo, 5s.

THE INTERNATIONAL SCIENTIFIC SERIES.

I. **Forms of Water:** a Familiar Exposition of the Origin and Phenomena of Glaciers. By J. Tyndall, LL.D., F.R.S. With 25 Illustrations. Eighth Edition. Crown 8vo, 5s.

II. **Physics and Politics;** or, Thoughts on the Application of the Principles of "Natural Selection" and "Inheritance" to Political Society. By Walter Bagehot. Fifth Edition. Crown 8vo, 4s.

III. **Foods.** By Edward Smith, M.D., LL.B., F.R.S. With numerous Illustrations. Seventh Edition. Crown 8vo, 5s.

IV. **Mind and Body:** the Theories of their Relation. By Alexander Bain, LL.D. With Four Illustrations. Seventh Edition. Crown 8vo, 4s.

V. **The Study of Sociology.** By Herbert Spencer. Tenth Edition. Crown 8vo, 5s.

VI. **On the Conservation of Energy.** By Balfour Stewart, M.A., LL.D., F.R.S. With 14 Illustrations. Fifth Edition. Crown 8vo, 5s.

VII. **Animal Locomotion**; or Walking, Swimming, and Flying. By J. B. Pettigrew, M.D., F.R.S., etc. With 130 Illustrations. Second Edition. Crown 8vo, 5s.

VIII. **Responsibility in Mental Disease.** By Henry Maudsley, M.D. Fourth Edition. Crown 8vo, 5s.

IX. **The New Chemistry.** By Professor J. P. Cooke. With 31 Illustrations. Sixth Edition. Crown 8vo, 5s.

X. **The Science of Law.** By Professor Sheldon Amos. Fifth Edition. Crown 8vo, 5s.

XI. **Animal Mechanism**: a Treatise on Terrestrial and Aerial Locomotion. By Professor E. J. Marey. With 117 Illustrations. Second Edition. Crown 8vo, 5s.

XII. **The Doctrine of Descent and Darwinism.** By Professor Oscar Schmidt. With 26 Illustrations. Fourth Edition. Crown 8vo, 5s.

XIII. **The History of the Conflict between Religion and Science.** By J. W. Draper, M.D., LL.D. Fifteenth Edition. Crown 8vo, 5s.

XIV. **Fungi**: their Nature, Influences, Uses, etc. By M. C. Cooke, M.D., LL.D. Edited by the Rev. M. J. Berkeley, M.A., F.L.S. With numerous Illustrations. Second Edition. Crown 8vo, 5s.

XV. **The Chemical Effects of Light and Photography.** By Dr. Hermann Vogel. Translation thoroughly revised. With 100 Illustrations. Third Edition. Crown 8vo, 5s.

XVI. **The Life and Growth of Language.** By Professor William Dwight Whitney. Third Edition. Crown 8vo, 5s.

XVII. **Money and the Mechanism of Exchange.** By W. Stanley Jevons, M.A., F.R.S. Fifth Edition. Crown 8vo, 5s.

XVIII. **The Nature of Light.** With a General Account of Physical Optics. By Dr. Eugene Lommel. With 188 Illustrations and a Table of Spectra in Chromo-lithography. Third Edition. Crown 8vo, 5s.

XIX. **Animal Parasites and Messmates.** By Monsieur Van Beneden. With 83 Illustrations. Second Edition. Crown 8vo, 5s.

XX. **Fermentation.** By Professor Schützenberger. With 28 Illustrations. Third Edition. Crown 8vo, 5s.

XXI. **The Five Senses of Man.** By Professor Bernstein. With 91 Illustrations. Third Edition. Crown 8vo, 5s.

XXII. **The Theory of Sound in its Relation to Music.** By Professor Pietro Blaserna. With numerous Illustrations. Second Edition. Crown 8vo, 5s.

XXIII. **Studies in Spectrum Analysis.** By J. Norman Lockyer, F.R.S. With six photographic Illustrations of Spectra, and numerous engravings on Wood. Crown 8vo. Second Edition. 6s. 6d.

Kegan Paul, Trench & Co.'s Publications. 29

XXIV. **A History of the Growth of the Steam Engine.** By Professor R. H. Thurston. With numerous Illustrations. Second Edition. Crown 8vo, 6s. 6d.

XXV. **Education as a Science.** By Alexander Bain, LL.D. Fourth Edition. Crown 8vo, 5s.

XXVI. **The Human Species.** By Professor A. de Quatrefages. Third Edition. Crown 8vo, 5s.

XXVII. **Modern Chromatics.** With Applications to Art and Industry. By Ogden N. Rood. With 130 original Illustrations. Second Edition. Crown 8vo, 5s.

XXVIII. **The Crayfish:** an Introduction to the Study of Zoology. By Professor T. H. Huxley. With 82 Illustrations. Third Edition. Crown 8vo, 5s.

XXIX. **The Brain as an Organ of Mind.** By H. Charlton Bastian, M.D. With numerous Illustrations. Second Edition. Crown 8vo, 5s.

XXX. **The Atomic Theory.** By Prof. Wurtz. Translated by G. Cleminshaw, F.C.S. Third Edition. Crown 8vo, 5s.

XXXI. **The Natural Conditions of Existence as they affect Animal Life.** By Karl Semper. With 2 Maps and 106 Woodcuts. Second Edition. Crown 8vo, 5s.

XXXII. **General Physiology of Muscles and Nerves.** By Prof. J. Rosenthal. Second Edition. With Illustrations. Crown 8vo, 5s.

XXXIII. **Sight:** an Exposition of the Principles of Monocular and Binocular Vision. By Joseph le Conte, LL.D. With 132 Illustrations. Crown 8vo, 5s.

XXXIV. **Illusions:** a Psychological Study. By James Sully. Second Edition. Crown 8vo, 5s.

XXXV. **Volcanoes:** what they are and what they teach. By Professor J. W. Judd, F.R.S. With 92 Illustrations on Wood. Second Edition. Crown 8vo, 5s.

XXXVI. **Suicide:** an Essay in Comparative Moral Statistics. By Prof. E. Morselli. With Diagrams. Crown 8vo, 5s.

XXXVII. **The Brain and its Functions.** By J. Luys. With Illustrations. Crown 8vo, 5s.

XXXVIII. **Myth and Science:** an Essay. By Tito Vignoli. Crown 8vo, 5s.

XXXIX. **The Sun.** By Professor Young. With Illustrations. Second Edition. Crown 8vo, 5s.

XL. **Ants, Bees, and Wasps:** a Record of Observations on the Habits of the Social Hymenoptera. By Sir John Lubbock, Bart., M.P. With 5 Chromo-lithographic Illustrations. Third Edition. Crown 8vo, 5s.

XLI. **Animal Intelligence.** By G. J. ROMANES, LL.D., F.R.S
Crown 8vo, 5*s*.

XLII. **The Concepts and Theories of Modern Physics.** By
J. B. STALLO. Crown 8vo, 5*s*.

MILITARY WORKS.

Army of the North German Confederation : a Brief Description of its Organisation, of the Different Branches of the Service and their *rôle* in War, of its Mode of Fighting, etc. Translated from the Corrected Edition, by permission of the Author, by Colonel Edward Newdigate. Demy 8vo, 5*s*.

BARRINGTON, Capt. J. T.—**England on the Defensive** ; or, the Problem of Invasion Critically Examined. Large crown 8vo with Map, 7*s*. 6*d*.

BLUME, Major W.—**The Operations of the German Armies in France**, from Sedan to the end of the War of 1870–71. With Map. From the Journals of the Head-quarters Staff. Translated by the late E. M. Jones, Maj. 20th Foot, Prof. of Mil. Hist. Sandhurst. Demy 8vo, 9*s*.

BOGUSLAWSKI, Capt. A. von.—**Tactical Deductions from the War of 1870-1.** Translated by Colonel Sir Lumley Graham Bart., late 18th (Royal Irish) Regiment. Third Edition, Revised and Corrected. Demy 8vo, 7*s*.

BRACKENBURY, Col. C. B., R.A., C.B.—**Military Handbook for Regimental Officers.** I. Military Sketching and Reconnaissance, by Lieut.-Col. F. J. Hutchison, and Capt. H. G. MacGregor. Fourth Edition. With 15 Plates. Small 8vo, 6*s*. II The Elements of Modern Tactics Practically applied to English Formations, by Lieut-Col. Wilkinson Shaw. Fourth Edition With 25 Plates and Maps. Small crown 8vo, 9*s*.

BRIALMONT, Col. A.—**Hasty Intrenchments.** Translated by Lieut. Charles A. Empson, R.A. With Nine Plates. Demy 8vo, 6*s*.

CLERY, C., Lieut.-Col.—**Minor Tactics.** With 26 Maps and Plans. Fifth and revised Edition. Demy 8vo, 16*s*.

DU VERNOIS, Col. von Verdy.—**Studies in Leading Troops** An authorised and accurate Translation by Lieutenant H. J. T Hildyard, 71st Foot. Parts I. and II. Demy 8vo, 7*s*.

GOETZE, Capt. A. von.—**Operations of the German Engineer during the War of 1870-1.** Published by Authority, and in accordance with Official Documents. Translated from the German by Colonel G. Graham, V.C., C.B., R.E. With 6 large Maps. Demy 8vo, 21*s*.

Kegan Paul, Trench & Co.'s Publications. 31

HARRISON, Lieut.-Col. R.—The Officer's Memorandum Book for Peace and War. Third Edition. Oblong 32mo, roan, with pencil, 3s. 6d.

HELVIG, Capt. H.—The Operations of the Bavarian Army Corps. Translated by Captain G. S. Schwabe. With 5 large Maps. In 2 vols. Demy 8vo, 24s.

Tactical Examples: Vol. I. The Battalion, 15s. Vol. II. The Regiment and Brigade, 10s. 6d. Translated from the German by Col. Sir Lumley Graham. With nearly 300 Diagrams. Demy 8vo.

HOFFBAUER, Capt.—The German Artillery in the Battles near Metz. Based on the Official Reports of the German Artillery. Translated by Captain E. O. Hollist. With Map and Plans. Demy 8vo, 21s.

LAYMANN, Capt.—The Frontal Attack of Infantry. Translated by Colonel Edward Newdigate. Crown 8vo, 2s. 6d.

Notes on Cavalry Tactics, Organisation, etc. By a Cavalry Officer. With Diagrams. Demy 8vo, 12s.

PARR, Capt. H. Hallam, C.M.G.—The Dress, Horses, and Equipment of Infantry and Staff Officers. Crown 8vo, 1s.

SCHAW, Col. H.—The Defence and Attack of Positions and Localities. Second Edition, revised and corrected. Crown 8vo, 3s. 6d.

SCHELL, Maj. von.—The Operations of the First Army under Gen. von Goeben. Translated by Col. C. H. von Wright. Four Maps. Demy 8vo, 9s.

The Operations of the First Army under Gen. von Steinmetz. Translated by Captain E. O. Hollist. Demy 8vo, 10s. 6d.

SCHELLENDORF, Major-Gen. B. von.—The Duties of the General Staff. Translated from the German by Lieutenant Hare. Vol. I. Demy 8vo, 10s. 6d.

SCHERFF, Maj. W. von.—Studies in the New Infantry Tactics. Parts I. and II. Translated from the German by Colonel Lumley Graham. Demy 8vo, 7s. 6d.

SHADWELL, Maj.-Gen., C.B.—Mountain Warfare. Illustrated by the Campaign of 1799 in Switzerland. Being a Translation of the Swiss Narrative compiled from the Works of the Archduke Charles, Jomini, and others. Also of Notes by General H. Dufour on the Campaign of the Valtelline in 1635. With Appendix, Maps, and Introductory Remarks. Demy 8vo, 16s.

SHERMAN, Gen. W. T.—Memoirs of General W. T. Sherman, Commander of the Federal Forces in the American Civil War. By Himself. 2 vols. With Map. Demy 8vo, 24s. *Copyright English Edition.*

STUBBS, Lieut.-Col. F. W.—**The Regiment of Bengal Artillery.** The History of its Organisation, Equipment, and War Services. Compiled from Published Works, Official Records, and various Private Sources. With numerous Maps and Illustrations. 2 vols. Demy 8vo, 32*s.*

STUMM, Lieut. Hugo.—**Russia's Advance Eastward.** Based on Official Reports. Translated by Capt. C. E. H. VINCENT. With Map. Crown 8vo, 6*s.*

VINCENT, Capt. C. E. H.—**Elementary Military Geography, Reconnoitring, and Sketching.** Compiled for Non-commissioned Officers and Soldiers of all Arms. Square crown 8vo, 2*s.* 6*d.*

Volunteer, the Militiaman, and the Regular Soldier. By a Public Schoolboy. Crown 8vo, 5*s.*

WARTENSLEBEN, Count H. von.—**The Operations of the South Army in January and February, 1871.** Compiled from the Official War Documents of the Head-quarters of the Southern Army. Translated by Colonel C. H. von Wright. With Maps. Demy 8vo, 6*s.*

The Operations of the First Army under Gen. von Manteufel. Translated by Col. C. H. von Wright. Uniform with the above. Demy 8vo, 9*s.*

WICKHAM, Capt. E. H., R.A.—**Influence of Firearms upon Tactics:** Historical and Critical Investigations. By an OFFICER OF SUPERIOR RANK (in the German Army). Translated by Captain E. H. Wickham, R.A. Demy 8vo, 7*s.* 6*d.*

WOINOVITS, Capt. I.—**Austrian Cavalry Exercise.** Translated by Captain W. S. Cooke. Crown 8vo, 7*s.*

POETRY.

ADAMS, W. D.—**Lyrics of Love,** from Shakspeare to Tennyson. Selected and arranged by. Fcap. 8vo, extra, gilt edges, 3*s.* 6*d.*

ADAM OF ST. VICTOR.—**The Liturgical Poetry of Adam of St. Victor.** From the text of Gautier. With Translations into English in the Original Metres, and Short Explanatory Notes, by Digby S. Wrangham, M.A. 3 vols. Crown 8vo, printed on hand-made paper, boards, 21*s.*

Antiope: a Tragedy. Large crown 8vo, 6*s.*

AUBERTIN, J. J.—**Camoens' Lusiads.** Portuguese Text, with Translation. Map and Portraits. 2 vols. Demy 8vo, 30*s.*

Seventy Sonnets of Camoens. Portuguese Text and Translation, with some original Poems. Dedicated to Capt. Richard F. Burton. Printed on hand-made paper, bevelled boards, gilt top, 7*s.* 6*d.*

AUCHMUTY, A. C.—**Poems of English Heroism** : From Brunanburh to Lucknow; from Athelstan to Albert. Small crown 8vo, 1s. 6d.

AVIA.—**The Odyssey of Homer.** Done into English Verse by. Fcap. 4to, 15s.

BANKS, Mrs. G. L.—**Ripples and Breakers:** Poems. Square 8vo, 5s.

BARNES, William.—**Poems of Rural Life, in the Dorset Dialect.** New Edition, complete in one vol. Crown 8vo, 8s. 6d.

BAYNES, Rev. Canon H. R.—**Home Songs for Quiet Hours.** Fourth and cheaper Edition. Fcap 8vo, cloth, 2s. 6d.

** This may also be had handsomely bound in morocco with gilt edges.

BENNETT, Dr. W. C.—**Narrative Poems and Ballads.** Fcap. 8vo, sewed in coloured wrapper, 1s.

Songs for Sailors. Dedicated by Special Request to H.R.H. the Duke of Edinburgh. With Steel Portrait and Illustrations. Crown 8vo, 3s. 6d.

An Edition in Illustrated Paper Covers, 1s.

Songs of a Song Writer. Crown 8vo, 6s.

BEVINGTON, L. S.—**Key Notes.** Small crown 8vo, 5s.

BILLSON, C. J.—**The Acharnians of Aristophanes.** Crown 8vo, 3s. 6d.

BOWEN, H. C., M.A.—**Simple English Poems.** English Literature for Junior Classes. In Four Parts. Parts I., II., and III., 6d. each, and Part IV., 1s.

BRYANT, W. C.—**Poems.** Red-line Edition. With 24 Illustrations and Portrait of the Author. Crown 8vo, extra, 7s. 6d.

A Cheap Edition, with Frontispiece. Small crown 8vo, 3s. 6d.

BYRNNE, E. Fairfax.—**Milicent:** a Poem. Small crown 8vo, 6s.

Calderon's Dramas: the Wonder-Working Magician — Life is a Dream—the Purgatory of St. Patrick. Translated by Denis Florence MacCarthy. Post 8vo, 10s.

Chronicles of Christopher Columbus. A Poem in 12 Cantos. By M. D. C. Small crown 8vo.

CLARKE, Mary Cowden.—**Honey from the Weed.** Verses. Crown 8vo, 7s.

COLOMB, Colonel.—**The Cardinal Archbishop:** a Spanish Legend. In 29 Cancions. Small crown 8vo, 5s.

CONWAY, Hugh.—**A Life's Idylls.** Small crown 8vo, 3s. 6d.

COPPÉE, Francois.—**L'Exilée.** Done into English Verse, with the sanction of the Author, by I. O. L. Crown 8vo, vellum, 5s.

DAVIES, T. Hart.—**Catullus.** Translated into English Verse. Crown 8vo, 6s.

DE VERE, Aubrey.—**The Foray of Queen Meave, and other** Legends of Ireland's Heroic Age. Small crown 8vo, 5s.

Alexander the Great: a Dramatic Poem. Small crown 8vo, 5s.

The Legends of St. Patrick, and other Poems. Small crown 8vo, 5s.

St. Thomas of Canterbury: a Dramatic Poem. Large fcap. 8vo, 5s.

Legends of the Saxon Saints. Small crown 8vo, 6s.

Antar and Zara: an Eastern Romance. Inisfail, and other Poems, Meditative and Lyrical. Fcap. 8vo, 6s.

The Fall of Rora, The Search after Proserpine, and other Poems, Meditative and Lyrical. Fcap. 8vo, 6s.

The Infant Bridal, and other Poems. A New and Enlarged Edition. Fcap. 8vo, 7s. 6d.

DOBELL, Mrs. Horace.—**Ethelstone, Eveline, and other Poems.** Crown 8vo, 6s.

DOBSON, Austin.—**Vignettes in Rhyme,** and Vers de Société. Third Edition. Fcap. 8vo, 5s.

Proverbs in Porcelain. By the Author of "Vignettes in Rhyme." Second Edition. Crown 8vo, 6s.

Dorothy: a Country Story in Elegiac Verse. With Preface. Demy 8vo, 5s.

DOWDEN, Edward, LL.D.—**Poems.** Second Edition. Fcap. 8vo, 5s.

Shakspere's Sonnets. With Introduction. Large post 8vo, 7s. 6d.

DOWNTON, Rev. H., M.A.—**Hymns and Verses.** Original and Translated. Small crown 8vo, 3s. 6d.

DUTT, Toru.—**A Sheaf Gleaned in French Fields.** New Edition, with Portrait. Demy 8vo, 10s. 6d.

Ancient Ballads and Legends of Hindustan. With an Introductory Memoir by Edmund W. Gosse. Small crown 8vo, printed on hand-made paper, 5s.

EDWARDS, Rev. Basil.—**Minor Chords**; or, Songs for the Suffering: a Volume of Verse. Fcap. 8vo, 3s. 6d.; paper, 2s. 6d.

ELDRYTH, Maud.—**Margaret, and other Poems.** Small crown 8vo, 3s. 6d.

ELLIOTT, Ebenezer, The Corn Law Rhymer.—**Poems.** Edited by his son, the Rev. Edwin Elliott, of St. John's, Antigua. 2 vols. Crown 8vo, 18s.

Kegan Paul, Trench & Co.'s Publications.

English Odes. Selected, with a Critical Introduction by EDMUND W. GOSSE, and a miniature frontispiece by Hamo Thornycroft, A.R.A. Elzevir 8vo, limp parchment antique, 6s.; vellum, 7s. 6d.

Epic of Hades, The. By the Author of "Songs of Two Worlds." Thirteenth Edition. Fcap. 8vo, 7s. 6d.

*** Also an Illustrated Edition, with 17 full-page designs in photo-mezzotint by George R. Chapman. 4to, extra, gilt leaves, 25s.; and a Large Paper Edition, with Portrait, 10s. 6d.

EVANS, Anne.—**Poems and Music.** With Memorial Preface by ANN THACKERAY RITCHIE. Large crown 8vo, 7s.

GOSSE, Edmund W.—**New Poems.** Crown 8vo, 7s. 6d.

GROTE, A. R.—**Rip van Winkle:** a Sun Myth; and other Poems. Small crown 8vo, printed on hand-made paper, limp parchment antique, 5s.

GURNEY, Rev. Alfred.—**The Vision of the Eucharist,** and other Poems. Crown 8vo, 5s.

Gwen: a Drama in Monologue. By the Author of the "Epic of Hades." Third Edition. Fcap. 8vo, 5s.

HAWKER, Robt. Stephen.—**The Poetical Works of.** Now first collected and arranged. With a Prefatory Notice by J. G. Godwin. With Portrait. Crown 8vo, 12s.

HELLON, H. G.—**Daphnis:** a Pastoral Poem. Small crown 8vo, 3s. 6d.

HICKEY, E. H.—**A Sculptor,** and other Poems. Small crown 8vo, 5s.

HOLMES, E. G. A.—**Poems.** First and Second Series. Fcap. 8vo, 5s. each.

Horati Opera. Edited by F. A. CORNISH, Assistant Master at Eton. With a Frontispiece after a design by L. Alma Tadema, etched by Leopold Lowenstam. Parchment Library Edition, 6s.; vellum, 7s. 6d.

INGHAM, Sarson, C. J.—**Cædmon's Vision, and other Poems.** Small crown 8vo, 5s.

JENKINS, Rev. Canon.—**The Girdle Legend of Prato.** Small crown 8vo, 2s.

Alfonso Petrucci, Cardinal and Conspirator: an Historical Tragedy in Five Acts. Small crown 8vo, 3s. 6d.

KING, Mrs. Hamilton.—**The Disciples.** Fourth Edition, with Portrait and Notes. Crown 8vo, 7s. 6d.

Aspromonte, and other Poems. Second Edition. Fcap. 8vo,

LANG, A.—**XXXII Ballades in Blue China.** Elzevir 8vo, parchment, 5s.

LEIGH, Arran and Isla.—**Bellerophon.** Small crown 8vo, 5s.

LEIGHTON, Robert.—**Records,** and other Poems. With Portrait. Small crown 8vo, 7s. 6d.

LOCKER, F.—**London Lyrics.** A New and Revised Edition, with Additions and a Portrait of the Author. Crown 8vo, 6s.

*** Also a New and Cheaper Edition. Small crown 8vo, 2s. 6d.

Love Sonnets of Proteus. With Frontispiece by the Author. Elzevir 8vo, 5s.

LOWNDES, Henry.—**Poems and Translations.** Crown 8vo, 6s.

LUMSDEN, Lieut.-Col. H. W.—**Beowulf :** an Old English Poem. Translated into Modern Rhymes. Small crown 8vo, 5s.

MACLEAN, Charles Donald.—**Latin and Greek Verse Translations.** Small crown 8vo, 2s.

MAGNUSSON, Eirikr, M.A., and PALMER, E. H., M.A.—**Johan Ludvig Runeberg's Lyrical Songs, Idylls, and Epigrams.** Fcap. 8vo, 5s.

MEREDITH, Owen, The Earl of Lytton.—**Lucile.** With 160 Illustrations. Crown 4to, extra, gilt leaves, 21s.

MIDDLETON, The Lady.—**Ballads.** Square 16mo, 3s. 6d.

MOORE, Mrs. Bloomfield.—**Gondaline's Lesson :** The Warden's Tale, Stories for Children, and other Poems. Crown 8vo, 5s.

MORICE, Rev. F. D., M.A.—**The Olympian and Pythian Odes of Pindar.** A New Translation in English Verse. Crown 8vo, 7s. 6d.

MORSHEAD, E. D. A. — **The House of Atreus.** Being the Agamemnon, Libation-Bearers, and Furies of Æschylus. Translated into English Verse. Crown 8vo, 7s.

NADEN, Constance W.—**Songs and Sonnets of Spring Time.** Small crown 8vo, 5s.

NICHOLSON, Edward B.—**The Christ Child,** and other Poems. Crown 8vo, 4s. 6d.

NOAKE, Major R. Compton.—**The Bivouac ;** or, Martial Lyrist. With an Appendix : Advice to the Soldier. Fcap. 8vo, 5s. 6d.

NOEL, The Hon. Roden.—**A Little Child's Monument.** Second Edition. Small crown 8vo, 3s. 6d.

NORRIS, Rev. Alfred.—**The Inner and Outer Life Poems.** Fcap. 8vo, 6s.

Ode of Life, The. By the Author of "The Epic of Hades," etc. Fourth Edition. Crown 8vo, 5s.

Kegan Paul, Trench & Co.'s Publications. 37

O'HAGAN, John.—**The Song of Roland.** Translated into English Verse. Large post 8vo, parchment antique, 10s. 6d.

PAUL, C. Kegan.—**Goethe's Faust.** A New Translation in Rhyme. Crown 8vo, 6s.

PAYNE, John.—**Songs of Life and Death.** Crown 8vo, 5s.

PENNELL, H. Cholmondeley.—**Pegasus Resaddled.** By the Author of "Puck on Pegasus," etc., etc. With 10 Full-page Illustrations by George Du Maurier. Second Edition. Fcap. 4to, elegant, 12s. 6d.

PFEIFFER, Emily.—**Glan Alarch: His Silence and Song: a Poem.** Second Edition. Crown 8vo, 6s.

Gerard's Monument, and other Poems. Second Edition. Crown 8vo, 6s.

Quarterman's Grace, and other Poems. Crown 8vo, 5s.

Poems. Second Edition. Crown 8vo, 6s.

Sonnets and Songs. New Edition. 16mo, handsomely printed and bound in cloth, gilt edges, 4s.

Under the Aspens: Lyrical and Dramatic. With Portrait. Crown 8vo, 6s.

PIKE, Warburton.—**The Inferno of Dante Allighieri.** Demy 8vo, 5s.

POE, Edgar Allan.—**Poems.** With an Essay on his Poetry by ANDREW LANG, and a Frontispiece by Linley Sambourne. Parchment Library Edition, 6s.; vellum, 7s. 6d.

RHOADES, James.—**The Georgics of Virgil.** Translated into English Verse. Small crown 8vo, 5s.

ROBINSON, A. Mary F.—**A Handful of Honeysuckle.** Fcap. 8vo, 3s. 6d.

The Crowned Hippolytus. Translated from Euripides. With New Poems. Small crown 8vo, 5s.

Schiller's Mary Stuart. German Text, with English Translation on opposite page by LEEDHAM WHITE. Crown 8vo, 6s.

Shakspere's Sonnets. Edited by EDWARD DOWDEN. With a Frontispiece etched by Leopold Lowenstam, after the Death Mask. Parchment Library Edition, 6s.; vellum, 7s. 6d.

Shakspere's Works. In 12 Monthly Volumes. Parchment Library Edition, 6s. each; vellum, 7s. 6d. each.

SHELLEY, Percy Bysshe.—**Poems Selected from.** Dedicated to Lady Shelley. With Preface by Richard Garnett. Parchment Library Edition, 6s.; vellum, 7s. 6d.

Six Ballads about King Arthur. Crown 8vo, extra, gilt edges, ' 3s. 6d.

SKINNER, *James.*—Cœlestia. The Manual of St. Augustine. The Latin Text side by side with an English Interpretation in Thirty-six Odes with Notes, *and* a plea *for the* study *of* Mystical Theology. Large crown 8vo, 6s.

Songs of Two Worlds. By the Author of "The Epic of Hades." Seventh Edition. Complete in One Volume, with Portrait. Fcap. 8vo, 7s. 6d.

Songs for Music. By Four Friends. Containing Songs by Reginald A. Gatty, Stephen H. Gatty, Greville J. Chester, and Juliana Ewing. Square crown 8vo, 5s.

STEDMAN, *Edmund Clarence.*—Lyrics and Idylls, with other Poems. Crown 8vo, 7s. 6d.

STEVENS, *William.*—The Truce of God, and other Poems. Small crown 8vo, 3s. 6d.

TAYLOR, *Sir H.*—Works Complete in Five Volumes. Crown 8vo, 30s.

TENNYSON, *Alfred.*—Works Complete:—

The Imperial Library Edition. Complete in 7 vols. Demy 8vo, 10s. 6d. each; in Roxburgh binding, 12s. 6d. each.

Author's Edition. In 7 vols. Post 8vo, gilt 43s. 6d.; or half-morocco, Roxburgh style, 52s. 6d.

Cabinet Edition. 13 vols. Each with Frontispiece. Fcap. 8vo, 2s. 6d. each.

Cabinet Edition. 13 vols. Complete in handsome Ornamental Case. 35s.

The Royal Edition. In 1 vol. With 26 Illustrations and Portrait. Extra, bevelled boards, gilt leaves, 21s.

The Guinea Edition. Complete in 13 vols. neatly bound and enclosed in box, 21s.; French morocco or parchment, 31s. 6d.

Shilling Edition. In 13 vols. pocket size, 1s. each, sewed.

The Crown Edition. Complete in 1 vol. strongly bound, 6s.; extra gilt leaves, 7s. 6d.; Roxburgh, half-morocco, 8s. 6d.

_{*} Can also be had in a variety of other bindings.

"In Memoriam." With a Miniature Portrait in *eau-forte* by Le Rat, after a Photograph by the late Mrs. Cameron. Parchment Library Edition, 6s.; vellum, 7s. 6d.

The Princess. A Medley. With a Miniature Frontispiece by H. M. Paget, and a Tailpiece in Outline by Gordon Browne. Parchment Library Edition, 6s.; vellum, 7s. 6d.

Songs Set to Music by various Composers. Edited by W. J. Cusins. Dedicated, by express permission, to Her Majesty the Queen. Royal 4to, extra, gilt leaves, 21s.; or in half-morocco, 25s.

Kegan Paul, Trench & Co.'s Publications.

TENNYSON, Alfred.—*continued.*
Original Editions :—
Ballads, and other Poems. Small 8vo, 5s.
Poems. Small 8vo, 6s.
Maud, and other Poems. Small 8vo, 3s. 6d.
The Princess. Small 8vo, 3s. 6d.
Idylls of the King. Small 8vo, 5s.
Idylls of the King. Complete. Small 8vo, 6s.
The Holy Grail, and other Poems. Small 8vo, 4s. 6d.
Gareth and Lynette. Small 8vo, 3s.
Enoch Arden, etc. Small 8vo, 3s. 6d.
In Memoriam. Small 8vo, 4s.
Harold : a Drama. New Edition. Crown 8vo, 6s.
Queen Mary : a Drama. New Edition. Crown 8vo, 6s.
The Lover's Tale. Fcap. 8vo, 3s. 6d.
Selections from the above Works. Super royal 16mo. 3s. 6d.; gilt extra, 4s.
Songs from the above Works. 16mo. 2s. 6d. ; extra, 3s. 6d.
Idylls of the King, and other Poems. Illustrated by Julia Margaret Cameron. 2 vols. folio, half-bound morocco, £6 6s. each.
Tennyson for the Young and for Recitation. Specially arranged. Fcap. 8vo, 1s. 6d.
The Tennyson Birthday Book. Edited by Emily Shakespear. 32mo, limp, 2s. ; extra, 3s.
* A superior Edition, printed in red and black, on antique paper, specially prepared. Small crown 8vo, extra, gilt leaves, 5s. ; and in various calf and morocco bindings.
Horæ Tennysonianæ sive Eclogæ e Tennysono Latine Redditæ Cura A. J. Church, A.M. Small crown 8vo, 6s.

THOMPSON, Alice C.—Preludes : a Volume of Poems. Illustrated by Elizabeth Thompson (Painter of "The Roll Call "). 8vo, 7s. 6d.

THRING, Rev. Godfrey, B.A.—Hymns and Sacred Lyrics. Fcap. 8vo, 3s. 6d.

TODHUNTER, Dr. J.—Laurella, and other Poems. Crown 8vo, 6s. 6d.
Forest Songs. Small crown 8vo, 3s. 6d.
The True Tragedy of Rienzi : a Drama. 3s. 6d.
Alcestis : a Dramatic Poem. Extra fcap. 8vo, 5s.
A Study of Shelley. Crown 8vo, 7s.

40 A List of

Translations from Dante, Petrarch, Michael Angelo, and Vittoria Colonna. Fcap. 8vo, 7s. 6d.

TURNER, Rev. C. Tennyson.—Sonnets, Lyrics, and Translations. Crown 8vo, 4s. 6d.

    Collected Sonnets, Old and New. With Prefatory Poem by ALFRED TENNYSON; also some Marginal Notes by S. T. COLERIDGE, and a Critical Essay by JAMES SPEDDING. Fcap. 8vo, 7s. 6d.

WALTERS, Sophia Lydia.—The Brook: a Poem. Small crown 8vo, 3s. 6d.

    A Dreamer's Sketch Book. With 21 Illustrations by Percival Skelton, R. P. Leitch, W. H. J. BOOT, and T. R. PRITCHETT. Engraved by J. D. Cooper. Fcap. 4to, 12s. 6d.

WATERFIELD, W.—Hymns for Holy Days and Seasons. 32mo, 1s. 6d.

WAY, A., M.A.—The Odes of Horace Literally Translated in Metre. Fcap. 8vo, 2s.

WEBSTER, Augusta.—Disguises: a Drama. Small crown 8vo, 5s.

Wet Days. By a Farmer. Small crown 8vo, 6s.

WILKINS, William.—Songs of Study. Crown 8vo, 6s.

WILLOUGHBY, The Hon. Mrs.—On the North Wind—Thistledown: a Volume of Poems. Elegantly bound, small crown 8vo, 7s. 6d.

WOODS, James Chapman.—A Child of the People, and other Poems. Small crown 8vo, 5s.

YOUNG, Wm.—Gottlob, etcetera. Small crown 8vo, 3s. 6d.

YOUNGS, Ella Sharpe.—Paphus, and other Poems. Small crown 8vo, 3s. 6d.

WORKS OF FICTION IN ONE VOLUME.

BANKS, Mrs. G. L.—God's Providence House. New Edition. Crown 8vo, 3s. 6d.

BETHAM-EDWARDS, Miss M.—Kitty. With a Frontispiece. Crown 8vo, 6s.

Blue Roses; or, Helen Malinofska's Marriage. By the Author of "Véra." New and Cheaper Edition. With Frontispiece. Crown 8vo, 6s.

FRISWELL, J. Hain.—One of Two; or, The Left-Handed Bride. Crown 8vo, 3s. 6d.

GARRETT, E.—By Still Waters: a Story for Quiet Hours. With 7 Illustrations. Crown 8vo, 6s.

HARDY, Thomas.—**A Pair of Blue Eyes.** Author of "Far from the Madding Crowd." New Edition. Crown 8vo, 6s.

The Return of the Native. New Edition. With Frontispiece. Crown 8vo, 6s.

HOOPER, Mrs. G.—**The House of Raby.** Crown 8vo, 3s. 6d.

INGELOW, Jean.—**Off the Skelligs:** a Novel. With Frontispiece. Second Edition. Crown 8vo, 6s.

MACDONALD, G.—**Malcolm.** With Portrait of the Author engraved on Steel. Sixth Edition. Crown 8vo, 6s.

The Marquis of Lossie. Fourth Edition. With Frontispiece. Crown 8vo, 6s.

St. George and St. Michael. Third Edition. With Frontispiece. Crown 8vo, 6s.

MASTERMAN, J.—**Half-a-Dozen Daughters.** Crown 8vo, 3s. 6d.

MEREDITH, George.—**Ordeal of Richard Feverel.** New Edition. Crown 8vo, 6s.

The Egoist: A Comedy in Narrative. New and Cheaper Edition, with Frontispiece. Crown 8vo, 6s.

PALGRAVE, W. Gifford.—**Hermann Agha:** an Eastern Narrative. Third Edition. Crown 8vo, 6s.

Pandurang Hari; or, Memoirs of a Hindoo. With an Introductory Preface by Sir H. Bartle E. Frere, G.C.S.I., C.B. Crown 8vo, 6s.

PAUL, Margaret Agnes.—**Gentle and Simple;** a Story. New and Cheaper Edition, with Frontispiece. Crown 8vo, 6s.

SHAW, Flora L.—**Castle Blair;** a Story of Youthful Lives. New and Cheaper Edition, with Frontispiece. Crown 8vo, 6s.

STRETTON, Hesba.—**Through a Needle's Eye:** a Story. New and Cheaper Edition, with Frontispiece. Crown 8vo, 6s.

TAYLOR, Col. Meadows, C.S.I., M.R.I.A.—**Seeta:** a Novel. New and Cheaper Edition. With Frontispiece. Crown 8vo, 6s.

Tippoo Sultaun: a Tale of the Mysore War. New Edition, with Frontispiece. Crown 8vo, 6s.

Ralph Darnell. New and Cheaper Edition. With Frontispiece. Crown 8vo, 6s.

A Noble Queen. New and Cheaper Edition. With Frontispiece. Crown 8vo, 6s.

The Confessions of a Thug. Crown 8vo, 6s.

Tara: a Mahratta Tale. Crown 8vo, 6s.

THOMAS, Moy.—**A Fight for Life.** Crown 8vo, 3s. 6d.

Within Sound of the Sea. New and Cheaper Edition, with Frontispiece. Crown 8vo, 6s.

BOOKS FOR THE YOUNG.

Aunt Mary's Bran Pie. By the Author of "St. Olave's." Illustrated. 3s. 6d.

BARLEE, Ellen.—**Locked Out:** a Tale of the Strike. With a Frontispiece. Royal 16mo, 1s. 6d.

BONWICK, J., F.R.G.S.—**The Tasmanian Lily.** With Frontispiece. Crown 8vo, 5s.

    Mike Howe, the Bushranger of Van Diemen's Land. New and Cheaper Edition. With Frontispiece. Crown 8vo, 3s. 6d.

Brave Men's Footsteps. A Book of Example and Anecdote for Young People. By the Editor of "Men who have Risen." With 4 Illustrations by C. Doyle. Seventh Edition. Crown 8vo, 3s. 6d.

Children's Toys, and some Elementary Lessons in General Knowledge which they teach. Illustrated. Crown 8vo, 5s.

COLERIDGE, Sara.—**Pretty Lessons in Verse for Good Children,** with some Lessons in Latin, in Easy Rhyme. A New Edition. Illustrated. Fcap. 8vo, 3s. 6d.

D'ANVERS, N. R.—**Little Minnie's Troubles:** an Every-day Chronicle. With 4 Illustrations by W. H. Hughes. Fcap. 8vo, 3s. 6d.

    Parted: a Tale of Clouds and Sunshine. With 4 Illustrations. Extra fcap. 8vo, 3s. 6d.

    Pixie's Adventures; or, the Tale of a Terrier. With 21 Illustrations. 16mo, 4s. 6d.

    Nanny's Adventures: or, the Tale of a Goat. With 12 Illustrations. 16mo, 4s. 6d.

DAVIES, G. Christopher.—**Rambles and Adventures of our School Field Club.** With 4 Illustrations. New and Cheaper Edition. Crown 8vo, 3s. 6d.

DRUMMOND, Miss.—**Tripp's Buildings.** A Study from Life, with Frontispiece. Small crown 8vo, 3s. 6d.

EDMONDS, Herbert.—**Well Spent Lives:** a Series of Modern Biographies. New and Cheaper Edition. Crown 8vo, 3s. 6d.

EVANS, Mark.—**The Story of our Father's Love,** told to Children. Fourth and Cheaper Edition of Theology for Children. With Illustrations. Fcap. 8vo, 1s. 6d.

FARQUHARSON, M.
    I. **Elsie Dinsmore.** Crown 8vo, 3s. 6d.
    II. **Elsie's Girlhood.** Crown 8vo, 3s. 6d.
    III. **Elsie's Holidays at Roselands.** Crown 8vo, 3s. 6d.

HERFORD, Brooke.—**The Story of Religion in England:** a Book for Young Folk. Crown 8vo, 5s.

INGELOW, Jean.—The Little Wonder-horn. With 15 Illustrations. Small 8vo, 2s. 6d.

JOHNSON, Virginia W.—The Catskill Fairies. Illustrated by ALFRED FREDERICKS. 5s.

KER, David.—The Boy Slave in Bokhara: a Tale of Central Asia. With Illustrations. New and Cheaper Edition. Crown 8vo, 3s. 6d.

The Wild Horseman of the Pampas. Illustrated. New and Cheaper Edition. Crown 8vo, 3s. 6d.

LAMONT, Martha MacDonald.—The Gladiator: a Life under the Roman Empire in the beginning of the Third Century. With 4 Illustrations by H. M. Paget. Extra fcap. 8vo, 3s. 6d.

LEANDER, Richard.—Fantastic Stories. Translated from the German by Paulina B. Granville. With 8 Full-page Illustrations by M. E. Fraser-Tytler. Crown 8vo, 5s.

LEE, Holme.—Her Title of Honour. A Book for Girls. New Edition. With a Frontispiece. Crown 8vo, 5s.

LEWIS, Mary A.—A Rat with Three Tales. New and Cheaper Edition. With 4 Illustrations by Catherine F. Frere. 3s. 6d.

MACKENNA, S. J.—Plucky Fellows. A Book for Boys. With 6 Illustrations. Fifth Edition. Crown 8vo, 3s. 6d.

At School with an Old Dragoon. With 6 Illustrations. New and Cheaper Edition. Crown 8vo, 3s. 6d.

Mc CLINTOCK, L.—Sir Spangle and the Dingy Hen. Illustrated. Square crown 8vo, 2s. 6d.

MALDEN, H. E.—Princes and Princesses: Two Fairy Tales. Illustrated. Small crown 8vo, 2s. 6d.

Master Bobby. By the Author of "Christina North." With 6 Illustrations. Fcap. 8vo, 3s. 6d.

NAAKE, J. T.—Slavonic Fairy Tales. From Russian, Servian, Polish, and Bohemian Sources. With 4 Illustrations. Crown 8vo, 5s.

PELLETAN, E.—The Desert Pastor, Jean Jarousseau. Translated from the French. By Colonel E. P. De L'Hoste. With a Frontispiece. New Edition. Fcap. 8vo, 3s. 6d.

REANEY, Mrs. G. S.—Waking and Working; or, From Girlhood to Womanhood. New and Cheaper Edition. With a Frontispiece. Crown 8vo, 3s. 6d.

Blessing and Blessed: a Sketch of Girl Life. New and Cheaper Edition. Crown 8vo, 3s. 6d.

Rose Gurney's Discovery. A Book for Girls. Dedicated to their Mothers. Crown 8vo, 3s. 6d.

English Girls: Their Place and Power. With Preface by the Rev. R. W. Dale. Third Edition. Fcap. 8vo, 2s. 6d.

REANEY, Mrs. G. S.—continued.
> **Just Anyone,** and other Stories. Three Illustrations. Royal 16mo, 1s. 6d.
>
> **Sunbeam Willie,** and other Stories. Three Illustrations. Royal 16mo, 1s. 6d.
>
> **Sunshine Jenny,** and other Stories. Three Illustrations. Royal 16mo, 1s. 6d.

ROSS, Mrs. E. ("Nelsie Brook")—**Daddy's Pet.** A Sketch from Humble Life. With 6 Illustrations. Royal 16mo, 1s.

SADLER, S. W., R.N.—**The African Cruiser:** a Midshipman's Adventures on the West Coast. With 3 Illustrations. New and Cheaper Edition. Crown 8vo, 2s. 6d.

Seeking his Fortune, and other Stories. With 4 Illustrations. New and Cheaper Edition. Crown 8vo, 2s. 6d.

Seven Autumn Leaves from Fairy Land. Illustrated with 9 Etchings. Square crown 8vo, 3s. 6d.

STOCKTON, Frank R.—**A Jolly Fellowship.** With 20 Illustrations. Crown 8vo, 5s.

STORR, Francis, and TURNER, Hawes.—**Canterbury Chimes;** or, Chaucer Tales retold to Children. With 6 Illustrations from the Ellesmere MS. Second Edition. Fcap. 8vo, 3s. 6d.

STRETTON, Hesba.—**David Lloyd's Last Will.** With 4 Illustrations. New Edition. Royal 16mo, 2s. 6d.

> **The Wonderful Life.** Sixteenth Thousand. Fcap. 8vo, 2s. 6d.

Sunnyland Stories. By the Author of "Aunt Mary's Bran Pie." Illustrated. Second Edition. Small 8vo, 3s. 6d.

Tales from Ariosto Re-told for Children. By a Lady. With 3 Illustrations. Crown 8vo, 4s. 6d.

WHITAKER, Florence.—**Christy's Inheritance.** A London Story. Illustrated. Royal 16mo, 1s. 6d.

ZIMMERN, H.—**Stories in Precious Stones.** With 6 Illustrations. Third Edition. Crown 8vo, 5s.

www.ingramcontent.com/pod-product-compliance
Lightning Source LLC
Chambersburg PA
CBHW032228230426
43666CB00033B/1635